Living With Autism Undiagnosed

R. Horowitz

On the Spectrum Press—Socorro, NM
Title: *Living With Autism Undiagnosed*
Author: R. Horowitz
Digital distribution | 2024
Paperback | 2024

Dedication

This book is dedicated to all the undiagnosed autistics, past, present, and future. I hear you!

Introduction

For decades autism was thought to mainly afflict white boys. Approximately four times as many boys were diagnosed with autism compared to girls. Recently that gap has narrowed significantly, and will most likely continue to narrow until it becomes nonexistent. Not because autism is suddenly becoming more prevalent in girls, but because, the medical community is getting better at diagnosing it in girls. However, that decades long oversight left many autistic girls undiagnosed, often misdiagnosed, struggling to get through life, often feeling like aliens from another planet, doing their best to comprehend the world around them, fit in as best they can, and failing, over and over. I am one of those girls.

My motivation for writing my story, is not to victimize myself, or try to elicit undue sympathy from readers. Rather, my intent is to increase autism awareness and acceptance, and help other autistic girls, and women, who are undiagnosed, recognize their autism. Since my diagnosis I have come to understand myself in ways I never thought possible. Had I known of my autism earlier my life outcomes might have been drastically better.

Being autistic in an allistic (non autistic) world is never easy, and being an undiagnosed autistic in an allistic world is significantly more difficult. Imagine you are participating in a play. Everyone has one script, you have a completely different script, and you have to try and figure out how your script is different from everyone else's in order to properly play your role. You do your best, even trying to sneak peeks at everyone else's script, but don't understand it. When you try to share your script with others they find it equally baffling. So you do your best, making mistakes and disrupting the play. Some of the actors try to be sympathetic, others just want you removed because you are ruining the play. Eventually you do get removed and have to go find another play. But it's hard to find another play because no one wants the actor with the different script. When you eventually get into another play the same thing keeps happening. These removals are analogous to losing a friend, a significant other, or a job. That's somewhat what it's like to be autistic in an allistic world. Now imagine you were never told you have a different script. You know something isn't right because you keep disrupting the play so you try really hard to figure out what you are doing wrong. You may even ask for clarifications from time to time but never get an answer, or get an answer you can't understand. Now you are getting removed from plays without even knowing why. No matter how hard you try you're never good enough. But, unlike the first scenario where you can explain to people that you have a different script, now you don't even know how to explain why you keep making mistakes. You are simply the bad actor who keeps messing up the play, and no one has any sympathy for you. That's what it's like to be an undiagnosed autistic in an allistic world. Suicide rates in autistic children and adults are thought to be 9 times higher than the rest of the population. I believe the actual number is much higher. How many of us die by suicide without ever getting diagnosed? If this book helps save even one life, it will have served its purpose, though I hope the impact will be greater.

As difficult as it is to be autistic in an allistic world, being autistic is not the tragedy the medical community portrays. Many of us are highly intelligent, talented, and capable of high achievement. Many high masking autistics are drawn to STEM fields because our hyper logical brains do well in those disciplines. What we need is to know we are autistic so we can understand ourselves, and our needs, as well as some basic accommodations to help us deal with our sensitivities, and communication challenges. Not because we are inherently flawed, but, because we have a different operating system, and the world is geared towards allistic operating systems. If the world operated on our terms allistic people would be struggling. If you try to run a MAC with windows software you will have serious problems and vice versa. We need software that matches our hardware.

I hope you will read the last section where I discuss how the autistic community can be helped. Because, realizing you are autistic is just one step. For many, getting the diagnosis, and getting the help they need are equally important and difficult. The focus is on autistic children. I am elated that autistic children are now getting diagnosed at higher rates and getting help, though often that help is misguided and sometimes harmful. We don't need to learn how to be less autistic, we need to learn how to communicate our needs so that allistics understand us, and to be accepted for who we are. In today's world autistics need to mask in order to achieve even a modicum of success. Masking takes a huge toll on us, and we often end up broken and suicidal. Because of the high suicide rate, the average life span of high masking autistics is 54. This is a tragedy that needs to be addressed. Society currently ignores the fact that autistic children grow into autistic adults who need services, accommodations, and acceptance.

I was fortunate to get diagnosed while I was in residential care. Many women self-diagnose and are unable to get the formal diagnosis for several reasons. Hardly anyone diagnoses adults. The rare clinics that do diagnose adults are prohibitively expensive. It costs thousands of dollars to get a diagnosis in the US, and most autistics can't afford to pay thousands of dollars. We struggle to hold jobs and are living paycheck to paycheck our entire lives. Not because we aren't competent, but because we don't fit in. Many are homeless. I have been homeless a few times in my life for short periods. Then there's the continued gender bias. Women are often still being evaluated the way men are. I was, but, luckily I am more classically autistic. Most autistic women have different presentations of autism. So even if a woman is able to find a location, and scrape together the money, she could get a non-autistic verdict even though she is autistic. Some women have managed to go through several evaluations before finding the right evaluator who is able to recognize her female autism expression. Very few autistic women have the means to go through this.

Autism is a spectrum, and each autistic person has their own struggles and talents. We have a saying in the autistic community, "If you have met one autistic person, you have met one autistic person."

My experiences are mine alone, and while I have found that many of my struggles are similar to those of other autistics, it cannot automatically be inferred that an autistic will face any of the same challenges I did, and many will face challenges I never had. I am just one voice in a sea of many. Please listen to us.

PART I
I'm Autistic

Chapter 1
I'm Autistic?

D r. R wants to see you, I was told. I was a little surprised because I had been told that, since I wasn't taking any medication, I would not be seeing her anymore during my stay. I was also intrigued, and somewhat pleased. I liked Dr. R. So I headed over to the clinic and set up a time to see her later that day. When I walked in she smiled at me and handed me some paperwork. "I'd like you to complete these assessments when you have the time and return them to me as soon as possible. We think you might be autistic." I was stunned. Autistic? Me? I had heard of Aspergers about two decades earlier and it had piqued my interest enough at the time to look it up, but had concluded that the profile didn't fit me for two reasons. First, I make eye contact, second, I have empathy. In fact, I tend to have too much empathy to the point where I forget my own needs and get swept up in others struggles. But I said none of this. "OK."

As I reviewed the questions on the autism assessment I became more and more cognizant of the fact that I was in fact autistic. I quickly completed the assessment and went back to the clinic but Dr. R was busy so I left her a message and went back to my cabin. A burning need for answers welled up in me and I went to sign up for some computer time so I could do some research. We were allowed 15 minutes at a time with a computer, so when I had the chance, I pulled up a bunch of articles and printed them out to take with me, and read in solitude. As I read the articles it became clearer and clearer that I was in fact autistic. It became overwhelming because for the first time in my 57 years, I felt like there was someone out there who could hear me. The tears wouldn't stop. Until that moment I hadn't fully realized just how lonely and misunderstood I felt. Because I had no answers I kept shoving those things aside, putting on a brave face for the world, and telling myself to let it go, that everything was fine.

***

You may be wondering why I didn't seek therapy for my problems. The fact is that I tried multiple times, and it never felt right. I never felt seen or heard by the therapist, and my instincts told me this wasn't what I needed. So I never went for more than a few sessions each time. I'm grateful now that I listened to my instincts. Most undiagnosed high masking autistic women end up getting diagnosed with either borderline personality disorder, bi-polar disorder, or schizophrenia when they seek therapy. Being misdiagnosed can be even worse than being undiagnosed because you are being treated for problems you don't have and these treatments whether therapy, medication, or both, can be very harmful. Autistics tend to be hyper sensitive to medication and can have severe complications from medication. I can't even handle over the counter pain killers anymore. The wrong therapy can be devastating because it doesn't work, and makes the person feel even worse. Even diagnosed autistics can end up in damaging therapy because so many therapists try to work with autistics without knowing enough about autism to help us. I have heard countless horror stories from other autistics, and have some of my own. It took me over six months to find the right therapist after I got diagnosed. I tried working with two others in the interim. The first was kind and supportive but it quickly became clear to me that he had no idea how to help me because he didn't understand autism. The second was so damaging that I couldn't even look for another therapist for several months.

***

Two days passed, and I had heard nothing back from Dr. R. My CPTSD (Complex Post Traumatic Stress Disorder) kicked in, and I started telling myself that I was worthless, and didn't even deserve to get a diagnosis. Every time I saw the paperwork sitting on the desk it seemed to be mocking me. Telling me how unworthy I was until I couldn't handle it anymore. I tore up the paperwork, and threw it in the garbage. Looking back, it wasn't a smart thing to do, but I was still highly suicidal, very emotionally fragile, and was incapable of coherent thinking when my CPSTSD was triggered. This is why I was in residential care. On top of that it was sending me into an autistic overwhelm, though I didn't know that at the time. My CPTSD triggers

3

would last for hours, sometimes even days. Except they didn't. The CPTSD trigger would send me into overwhelm. Depending on the circumstances the overwhelm could become a meltdown, and the meltdown could result in a shutdown. But at that time, I still had no understanding of all this.

Without the paperwork triggering me every few hours, I eventually calmed down enough, and headed back to the clinic to leave another message. I was told that Dr. R had simply been inundated with new admittances, and she would see me as soon as possible. When I finally got in to see her, I had to tell her what I had done, expecting to be handed a new assessment and told to come back later, but she just smiled and said, "If you have the time let's do it together now."

I happily agreed and while she tried to hide it, I could see her become more and more concerned as we went through the assessment with me making little comments like "well, to be honest I wouldn't want to go to either a party or a museum, but, if I had to pick one, it would be a museum." A score of 20 would indicate that I am autistic, some say the cutoff is 32, I scored 37.

"You mask very well," Dr. R told me. "It was very difficult to pick up on, but we finally managed to piece it all together. Now you can get the help you need."

I had so many questions, but couldn't seem to get any of them out.

"How are you feeling about this?" she asked me.

I admitted that it was a little overwhelming, and told her about the articles I had read. She nodded and gave some supportive platitudes. I walked out still wondering about the empathy, and eye contact, and what did "I mask very well" mean? I wanted this to be true because the more I researched autism, the clearer my life became to me, but I was afraid. I was afraid that if I brought it up I would be told, "well you can't be autistic if you have empathy and make eye contact," and all this sense of understanding would be snatched away from me. That fear stayed with me for about six weeks, until I finally came across a YouTube podcast, by an autistic man, that outlined ten misconceptions about autism. Two of those misconceptions were that all autistic people lack empathy, and that all autistic people do not make eye contact. Yes, the vast majority of autistic people do not make eye contact, but some do. Some autistic people struggle with empathy while others are hyper empathic. I was finally, wholeheartedly, able to accept the diagnosis, and dive deep into a journey of self-discovery,

4

understanding, acceptance, and grief over the life I could have had with an earlier diagnosis.

Unfortunately, those of us who are empathic still get labeled as "not empathetic" because of the double empathy problem. Autistic brains process information different than allistic brains, resulting in very different communication styles. We often end up saying things that sound rude, and/or insensitive to an allistic person, while we are trying to be supportive. At the same time, we find it very difficult to understand allistic people. Our communication style is very blunt, direct, and logic based. We often don't understand hidden meanings or nuance, and while many of us can feel empathy, many autistics have alexithymia, which is an inability to understand one's own feelings. Because we struggle to understand emotions, we tend to rely heavily on logic rather than emotions. I went through a period in my teens where I desperately wanted to be a Vulcan so I wouldn't have to deal with emotions. At best, an allistic person comes off to an autistic as incomprehensible and baffling, at worst, we think they lie all the time. This alone can create so much turmoil for an autistic that they isolate. I always get flustered when someone says, "how are you" to me. I have learned that I am not actually being asked how I am, and that the proper response is "fine thank you, how are you." But I don't understand why I am being asked how I am when the person asking doesn't actually want to know, and am disturbed at having to be duplicitous and say that I am fine when I'm not. That is just one example of the myriad of ways dealing with the allistic world taxes me.

Dr. R never told me how they had pieced it together, but, I believe I know what the missing piece that brought it all together for them was. During my first session with the EMDR therapist where we set up a "safe space" for me to go to when things got too overwhelming and, or, frightening, I was asked to provide a memory to work on in our next session. I had already decided on a memory. It wasn't my worst memory, but, it was my first memory of not being able to speak. I was hoping to resolve whatever was blocking me, and thought it might be related to that memory. Before I talk about it I want to emphasize that I have no animosity towards my parents for anything they have done to me over the years. I understand now that they have their own traumas, and psychological issues. This does not mean that what they did to me was right, it was simply understandable given the

5

things they were dealing with, and societal norms of that time. The more I unpack my own issues, the more I understand theirs.

When we lived in California my brothers and I attended a private Jewish school that ran from preschool to eighth grade. The nursery school was in a separate building and had regular household toilets. When I got to kindergarten at about age 5 we moved to the main building. The toilets were commercial and made significantly more noise when flushed. The sound of those toilets flushing sounded like bombs going off to me. I was terrified of them. So I started avoiding the bathroom while I was in school which led to wetting myself. My mother got very angry at me, and confronted me about this. I stood there with an explanation on the tip of my tongue, but no words would come out. As much as I wanted to explain, I was also afraid of her reaction if I told her the reason. She might beat me, and/or ridicule me more. After a few minutes she told me I was acting like a baby so she was going to treat me like a baby, and put me in diapers. I was still unable to speak. What if I told her and she mocked me even more and said that only babies are afraid of flushing toilets, or worse, she might beat me for being afraid of a flushing toilet. Even though the toilets had never exploded yet, that didn't mean they wouldn't ever, so the noise frightened me. The words would not come out of my mouth. I don't remember how long I was in diapers. I did eventually develop a system where I would be ready to leave the stall, open the door, reach for the handle from as far away as I could, and run for my life as soon as the toilet started flushing. As I grew older and learned to tune things out flushing toilets became more bearable to me, though I still struggle with the sound. I had never told anyone about this before because, I was too embarrassed about wetting myself, being put back in diapers, and about being afraid of the sound of a flushing toilet. But I decided to talk about it to try and resolve this inability to talk from time to time. It had become apparent to me as a serious problem I have over that last year. It doesn't only happen when I am afraid. This inability to speak at times is fairly common in the autistic community. Most people are aware that there are nonverbal autistics. Not many know that there are intermittently nonverbal autistics. The mechanism that drives this is very complex and not fully understood yet as far as I know, so I won't try and explain it. I don't always lose my ability to speak completely. Sometimes I get stuck saying the same thing over and over again, echolalia. This can be even more embarrassing in a professional or social setting.

I now know that being afraid of the sound of flushing toilets is a very common phenomenon with autistic children, and I believe that opening up about that memory, the inability to speak from time to time combined with my reaction to the sound of the flushing toilets led to my diagnosis. The social difficulties and my problems with food were already noted. I now know that this inability to speak at times is called selective mutism, though I prefer the term situational mutism as it has less negative connotations associated with it. Selective mutism sounds like a choice, but it isn't a choice. I wish I could control it.

I do believe that, had I been born in the 21st century I would have been diagnosed as a child. I was so shy and quiet, clumsy to the point of being comical. I couldn't catch a ball or do a simple somersault. As I got older games like jump rope, 5 stones (similar to jacks), and gumi where you had to go through a series of movements with a large elastic band were way too difficult for me to master. I have spent years improving my eye hand coordination and overall coordination and can now catch almost anything that is thrown at me. But I still can't do somersault, and I often drop things for no apparent reason.

Food issues have plagued me my whole life. Whenever I wanted to emphasize to people how 'weird' I am, I would tell them about my inability to eat ice cream when I was a child. Now, I finally understand all my food issues. I have heard other autistics describe their difficulties with food and I am not as bad some, though I do seem to have some odd grey areas with certain foods. My relationship with bananas is, well, bananas. Some days I can eat them, other days I can't. Sometimes I can eat a whole banana, some days I can only eat a bite or two. I will often enjoy a food for a period of time, then be completely unable to eat it for a period of time. Sometimes I lose the ability to ever eat it again. Growing up there were dishes my mother made that everyone else loved and I couldn't touch. Whenever she would fry something in butter I would be in agony from the smell. My parents thought I was just acting up with these, and many other things. Expressing my needs has led to labels such as difficult, needy, and demanding my entire life.

My social interaction issues are extremely complex. I always knew I had these difficulties. Too often I would say something and it would come back to me as something completely different from what I had said. I was constantly offending people for reasons I could not fathom.

I have often been labeled 'mean' when I was trying to be empathetic. I had convinced myself that I had these difficulties because I grew up in two different countries with very different cultures and didn't really fit in with either culture. This hypothesis was corroborated by others from dual cultures who admitted to having similar difficulties. I also tend to have fewer communication issues with Israelis as their communication style is more direct and straightforward. I did seem to have more difficulties than others with mixed backgrounds after I moved back to the US, but, I was also 'weird,' and that was a good enough explanation for me to shrug it all off. Oddly enough, up until my last break down, I was able to maintain self-esteem. I developed an attitude of "I like who I am and anyone who doesn't like me is missing out." But when I got the autism diagnosis all the nasty comments and judgements that I had brushed off over the years suddenly came home to roost. Even though I know there is nothing wrong with being autistic, I feel like there is a label on my forehead that people read as "defective." It's hard to have self-esteem when you are labeled defective.

Most importantly, I would have been diagnosed sooner because there is an increased awareness of autism in women. When I was born it was virtually impossible for a girl to get an autism diagnosis, and completely impossible for a high masking autistic to get diagnosed.

Chapter 2
Early memories

I was born on the east coast of the United States in the 1960's. When I was 8 months old my family moved to the west coast. I have no memory of these things, I know them anecdotally.

My earliest memory is being at a birthday party playing the farmer and the cheese. I was one of the youngest children there, about two and a half, because the party was for one of my older brothers' friends, and I ended up being the cheese. My mother claims that I started to cry when I was standing in the middle with everyone around me clapping and pointing at me. This makes sense to me now, because it probably put me in sensory overload even though I don't remember it. What I do remember is being told to close my eyes and count to ten. When I opened my eyes everyone was gone. I started to panic, ran around calling out to my mother and brother, but there was no response. I collapsed on the ground, and started to cry. As soon as I started crying everyone came out of their hiding places. They didn't realize I had no concept of hide and seek, and I had no idea that I had just had a meltdown.

My earliest memory of being beaten by my mother is from about age 3. Every Saturday the ice cream truck would come around. I could hear it from inside the house, but was not allowed to go to it because it was Saturday. My parents were orthodox and the rules were very strict. But there was a piece of candy I knew the ice cream truck had that I really wanted. So one Saturday I snuck out and went to buy it with the allowance money I had saved up. My mother caught me, dragged me home, and started beating me. I don't know how long it lasted I just remember screaming and screaming for what seemed like a very long time. Afterwards I crawled under my bed and refused to come out until late at night when everyone was asleep. I got very cold lying on the floor so I crawled into bed. I have no memory of this incident ever being discussed after that. I never told anyone about it until I was doing therapy for my CPTSD over fifty years later. I was too ashamed of what I had done.

We had a neighbor down the street I somehow became friendly with. For a while, maybe a year, I would go to their house regularly. They had no children, or, maybe their children were grown up. They did have a dog and they were nice to me. So I would go there as often as I could to spend time with them and play with the dog. I was approximately four at the time. Those visits are some of my happiest childhood memories. One day I came to their house and was told that my mother had said that I couldn't visit anymore. I could tell they were not happy about this, but there was nothing they could do, and nothing I could do. That was when I started to really resent my mother. She had taken away my happy place. But I was too afraid to talk to her about it.

I liked school, it was an escape from home, and the teachers were nice. I remember laughing really hard one day in nursery school. We were working on the Hebrew alphabet and had reached the letter Pei that has a sound like a P or an F depending on where it was in the word. We had been going over vowels and the teacher wrote on the blackboard *peepee* and *poopoo* in Hebrew. To a three year-old, it was hysterically funny. The whole class was laughing.

I didn't have many friends, the few I had were boys and they would come to my house and play dolls with me. There was the usual, I'll show you mine if you show me yours, and from time to time my brothers would try and get my playmate to play their rough and tumble games instead. I would get mad and tell them to find their own friends and leave mine alone. I had to share a room with them, I wasn't going to share my boyfriends with them. One day in kindergarten during nap time, I had placed my mat next to my current boyfriend's mat and we were whispering and giggling. For some reason the teacher only heard him, and made him stand in the corner. I felt bad, but not bad enough to say anything. After a little while I needed the restroom, and when I came back, I opened the door too forcefully and broke his nose. I cried more than he did and spent the rest of the afternoon telling him how sorry I was. He wasn't mad at me. It got him out of the corner, but I felt nothing but guilt over breaking his nose. It was my fault he was in the corner in the first place.

Our school was several miles from the house so my mother would drive us to school in the morning and pick us up in the afternoon. Sometimes my older brother and I would be playing in the yard and be late to meet her. She became increasingly angry each time this happened until she decided we needed to be punished. She told us we would have to walk home. I think I was in first grade because my younger brother was in nursery school which meant she would always pick him up first, he was already in the car. This means my older brother was in third grade. We were a little alarmed when she drove off but once we started walking we started enjoying ourselves. We played games like don't step on the crack, and Simon says as we made our way home. After a while, as we passed a familiar store, I remembered that I had my piggy bank in my bag. We decided to get some chocolate. We continued on our way happily munching on chocolate bars when my mother drove up. She was ANGRY! "Where have you been I've been worried sick about you, get in the car!"

We had both instinctively hid the chocolate behind our backs and said nothing as we got in the car. Our mouths were full of chocolate and it would be dangerous to say anything because she would see it. As she continued to yell at us about how irresponsible we were we shoved the rest of the chocolate in our mouths and swallowed it as fast as we could. We knew that if she found out about the chocolate she would get even angrier, and we might even get a beating.

On Sunday mornings when we knew our parents would be sleeping in, my brothers and I would get up early to play in the living room. We weren't allowed in the living room so we had to be careful. But it was the biggest room in the house with lots of furniture for us to hop around on. We always played the floor is lava tag. We would drag chairs to strategic positions and throw cushions on the floor to hop around on. As long as you didn't touch the actual floor you were safe. The moment we heard stirrings from the other side of the house we would quickly put everything away and run to our room. Maybe our parents knew what we were doing, but, based on their reactions to other things, I don't think they did.

For as long as I could remember my parents would talk about moving to Israel. They made it sound so exciting that by the time we actually moved we were all very hyped about it. I was seven at the time, and we started the trip in the summer, when the school year ended, and arrived in Israel when the next school year began in Israel, in September 1972. The plan was to stop in New York, visit family, then go to Europe for a month before arriving in Israel. I had never met any of my extended family. Suddenly we were meeting aunts, uncles. cousins, and grandparents. We spent most of the time at my father's sister's house. It was crowded, but I loved it there. I suddenly had the equivalent of three older sisters who doted on me. We all slept in a big bed in the attic while my parents and brothers slept in their room. We used flashlights to read late into the night under the covers, giggling over things I can't remember. I read Nancy Drew, The Bobsy Twins, The Secret Seven, and everything else in their library. I loved books and the house was a treasure trove for me. It is quite common for high masking autistics to have hyperlexia, and read at levels far above normal for their age.

I also met my mother's father for the first time. He and my grandmother were divorced. I have no recollection of meeting her at that time though I do remember meeting her a few years later. We even went to visit more distant relatives, I remember spending an afternoon sitting on the Satmer Rebbe's lap as he talked to my parents. My mother's family are Nadvorne Rebbe's and Nadvorne is an offshoot of Satmer, so we were fairly closely related. The irony of that memory is that Satmer opposes the existence of the modern state of Israel we were migrating to. They believe we need to wait for the Messiah to bring us back. At age seven I knew none of that.

We were having such a good time in New York that we ended up staying there and cancelling the trip to Europe. I never regretted that decision. While my uncle was a very quiet, uncommunicative and serious man, my aunt was sweet, bubbly and kind, the kind of mother I always wanted. From time to time jokingly threaten to beat me with a chapatchka (rug beater) when I misbehaved, but I knew she was joking because there was always a smile on her face and a twinkle in her eye when she would say it. I also knew she didn't have a chapatchka. Years later when I was in my twenties I bought her one in Israel and gave it to her as a gift during a visit. She was overwhelmed by that gift, continued to jokingly threaten me when I misbehaved, but never hit me with the chapatchka or anything else. She was very much like my father's mother I was told. Thinking back, I wish we had stayed there. But, at the time, the hype of Israel was so strong that I was excited when we finally set out on the final leg of the trip.

We arrived late at night. I remember waking up in my other aunt's home, but, I may have slept through the arrival because I have no memory of it. My aunt and uncle clearly had money but there was none of the warmth I felt in my New York aunt's home. I was also very disoriented, and it wasn't just jet lag. The milk was in a bag held up by a plastic container, and had strange white flecks in it. All the food containers were strange looking as was most of the food. I wanted cereal like I had at home, but the cereal was so different and unpalatable. I was still far from fluent in Hebrew and conversations were still difficult. My aunt and her family spoke English, but I never felt comfortable around them. Maybe it was the absence of other girls. My aunt in Israel had three boys. Maybe it was the underlying animosity between my mother and my aunt that would become more prominent as the years passed.

Within a few days we moved into a Maon Olim, a special motel for new immigrants. My mother complained nonstop the entire time we lived there. The constant yelling and fighting was very difficult for me to handle though I didn't fully understand the extent of my discomfort until I had received both my CPTSD and autism diagnosis. I just knew I was miserable. We stayed there for three months.

One girl at school took me around and introduced me to everyone, there was a culture of acceptance and trying to make new immigrants feel welcome in Israel. But it would take me years to feel comfortable there. My Hebrew wasn't good enough, and I struggled to become fluent enough to do well in school. I was also inept at the games they played in recess like gumi and five stones leading to more isolation. There were special lessons for new immigrant children during the first year, but, after that I was on my own, and I started to really struggle at school, stopped enjoying it, and withdrew. I expressed the need for more help but was told it wasn't available, I had used up my quota. My parents were unsupportive, I was intelligent enough, I should be able to manage without additional assistance. To them I was just being difficult. I became more and more withdrawn, and my schoolwork declined. I have no memory of anyone caring or asking what could be done to help me. I stopped caring about school. I lived in a world of fantasy driven by my passion for books, and my desire for parents who loved me. My most recurrent daydream was that I had been switched at birth and that my real parents would find me and take me home with them where they would love me, and dote on me. This type of daydream is very common for children raised in neglectful and abusive homes.

We visited my father's father while living in the Maon Olim. One of the reasons my parents picked that specific one was because it was a few blocks from the old people's home he lived in. I remember that first visit. It was my first time in a home like that and I didn't like it. It felt cold and unwelcoming. My grandfather spoke no English, and he was a very austere and domineering man with intelligent penetrating eyes that scared me. He and my father quickly got into an argument, and I withdrew into my daydreams wishing I could be somewhere else. I often wonder what it would have been like if my grandmother was still alive, but, she died when I was three, and I never got to meet her. I did hear a lot of stories about her. She was a lot like my New York aunt.

I visited my grandfather several more times while we lived in the Maon Olim, but the visits were always strained because of the language barrier, and I never developed a connection with him. He died when I was twelve after being sick in the hospital for a very long time. Children weren't allowed to visit in the hospital so I didn't see him that entire last year. I remember the day he died. I was at home because of a school holiday reading a book in my room. I heard the phone ring and immediately thought, Saba is dead. I slowly put the book down and dragged myself to the phone to answer it. I didn't want to hear it. When I finally picked up the phone my mother delivered the news I was expecting. I sat there for a long time trying to feel grief but it never came. Perhaps the lack of connection made it impossible to feel anything. Or, maybe, because this was my first intimate encounter with death I was too numb from overwhelm to process it. Or, maybe, it was a combination of both. All I remember is sitting there trying to pull up feelings of grief, and getting none. I wondered what was wrong with me. I was supposed to be grief stricken over the loss of a close family member but I wasn't. For years I felt shame and guilt over my lack of grief when he died. It still bothers me.

After three months in the Maon Olim we moved to a small apartment in a small town not too far from Tel Aviv. I started to enjoy the freedom of being able to walk to and from school on my own, but, other than that I was miserable. Since I had already been in the country for a few months no one felt the need to befriend me in my new school and I was unable to make friends on my own. Very shortly after the move I got my first pair of glasses, and the bullying started. I was completely on my own, so I withdrew even more into my world of fantasy.

After my attempt to get help with my language problems, I never

14

opened up to my parents about my problems at school. I had already learned that turning to them wasn't helpful at best, and could result in a beating at worst. As the years passed I became more closed off and more secretive about my whereabouts. Not because I felt there was anything wrong with what I was doing, but, because telling my parents anything was risky. The last time I shared an experience with my parents was when I was in high school. I had been to a classmate's house, and she told her parents about a prank the class had played on a teacher. Her parents laughed, and they joked about it the rest of the time I was there. Even though I had already learned to not share anything with my parents, seeing my friend's parents' reaction, I thought it would be safe to share the prank with my parents expecting them to react the same way. Instead, I got beaten for participating in the prank. I had not actually done anything, but they weren't listening. That was when I realized that no matter what, it was not safe to share anything with my parents.

About eight months after we moved from the Maon Olim the Yom Kippur war started, and life changed drastically. We were suddenly spending extended periods of time in bomb shelters. There were constant PSA's about preparing and storing provisions in bomb shelters, and about keeping buildings and roadways dark at night so the bombers wouldn't know what to target. We cut, and taped, black cardboard over all the windows, and were supposed to paint the car headlights with dark paint but my parents didn't want to do it. We weren't the only ones, so there were people going from block to block and parking lot to parking lot painting all the headlights. They eventually found our car and painted the headlights. For some reason my father ended up going back to the US for about year soon after the war started. My mother complained constantly about his absence and how difficult it was to be raising three children on her own. Then she would say that she equated it to women whose husbands were on the front. For some reason that last statement really bothered me, which is why I remember it so vividly. But it wasn't until I was an adult that I fully understood why.

**

I was eight years old (almost nine) when the war started, and while I had been introduced to the concept of death it was still quite removed from me. At the end of every news broadcast they would run the list

15

of fallen soldiers from that day. The lists were very long, and too much for me to process. I didn't unpack it until I was in residential care, right before I got my autism diagnosis. I joined a writing activity and the prompt was "it was late." I started writing about the first siren we heard on Yom Kippur, and going into the bomb shelter for the first time. As I wrote more memories came to me, including the suppressed memory of the lists of fallen soldiers I had watched every night. I wrote "Every night we would watch the list of fallen soldiers on the TV screen. Like movie credits, movie credits for actors who would never go home." When I read it out loud I started to cry uncontrollably, finally comprehending the tragedy of what I had seen. The loss of life, the lost potential, the broken families. It also allowed me to finally understand why my mother's comment was so upsetting. Yes she was on her own like the war wives, but, her husband was safe in another country, theirs were on the front, possibly never coming home.

***

Chapter 3
Perach

When I was ten we moved again, to a nearby town and a larger apartment. My new school was an all-girls school so the bullying stopped, and I made one friend. Her name was Perach (it means flower) and she lived a few blocks away from us. Her family had lived in the house for a long time and it was one of the few single dwelling homes in a sea of apartment buildings. They were not well off but were comfortable enough, though by US standards they would be considered poor. Both her parents were teachers and they accepted me with open arms into their home. Watching her family's dynamics, the love, kindness, and camaraderie, I started to realize there was something very wrong with my family. There was no kindness in my family, just put downs, and criticism. For as long as I can remember whenever my family would sit down to a meal together I ended up leaving the table crying. My father or older brother would start picking at me, then the other would join in. After a few minutes my younger brother would start throwing barbs at me. This would continue until I left the table crying, most likely in a meltdown. My older brother would then come to my room and tell me I was too sensitive and should stop being such a crybaby. Even when we were adults, this kept happening. My mother never joined in, but she didn't defend me, or intervene in anyway either. She just sat there in silence and let it happen, over, and over, and over again. The older I got the more I closed myself off from my family, refusing to fully accept their judgements of me, but they still hurt.

Because we lived so close, Perach and I would walk home from school together almost every day. It was a 20 minute walk that would take us about two hours. We would stop in every park, swing in every swing, sit on every bench and chat, pet every dog, make up songs, and just had a good time. Since my mother was working full time she had no idea what I was doing with my time, and didn't seem to care. I was free until she came home. After about a year we decided to write a book together. We both wanted it to be about a trip to Africa. I wanted there to be horses in the story and Perach wanted teachers in the story. We found a way to fit them both in. Whenever I would write I would focus on the horses and our adventures with them, and she would write about interactions with the teachers. It was a strange disjointed piece of literature, but, we had a lot of fun writing it. I still have the orange notebook we wrote in.

Perachs parents loved talking about how they met, and their dating days. Her mother was Iraqi and her father was Iranian. Back when they were dating 'mixed' marriages were uncommon, and when her parents started dating it created quite a stir. Iranians and Iraqis typically do not like each other, and these prejudices were imported to Israel when the Jewish communities immigrated there. Today no one cares, but back then, it was a very big deal. Perachs father would laugh about the fact that her mother's parents insisted she keep a knife in her purse on every date, and her mother would giggle every time he brought it up. It was in their eyes every time spoke of each other or looked at each other. They were clearly still very much in love. I don't remember Perach having any other friends in school. I wonder if her 'strange' mixed heritage made her something of an outcast which led to us forming such a close bond. Mixed marriages were just starting to become more prevalent in those days. Despite our close bond, Perach never came to my house, I always went to hers. I am not sure why that was but I was fine with it. Going to her house was an escape for me, and I had no desire for her to be dragged into my family's dynamics. The differences I saw in the dynamics between my family and Perachs family made me feel ashamed of my family. Perach's family was so warm and loving while mine was cold and denigrating. Not once, the entire time I was in my parents' house did I hear the words "I love you." Not to me, not to my brothers, and not between my parents. For a very long time I thought it was wrong to say I love you.

In eighth grade Perach and I became joint managers of the biology class petting zoo. There were mice, hamsters, guinea pigs, rabbits, a fish tank, turtles, tortoises, and pigeons. It was our job to keep the animals fed, the cages clean, and we had keys so we could come and go as needed. That was the year Anwar Sa'adat came to Israel to talk peace with Menachem Begin. The morning of the day he was arriving we found a dead rabbit in one of the cages. Perach jokingly suggested the rabbit died of a heart attack at the thought of Sa'adat coming to Israel. We laughed for days over that. The whole country was incredibly tense. The thought of a peace treaty was exhilarating, and very scary. If we signed a peace treaty, would the Egyptians honor it? I had my doubts, but have to admit that though tensions are often high, for 45 years Egypt has honored the treaty, and for that, I greatly respect them.

Chapter 4
High School

When we moved on to high school we went to different schools. Perach went to the local high school, and I went to an Ulpana (private religious school for girls) about twenty miles away. While we were in high school we still stayed in touch. I would walk over to her house almost every Saturday to spend time with her and her family. But the closeness we had those first few years was gone, and after high school we drifted apart. I went to her wedding, feeling totally out of place, and unsure of what to do or say to anyone. The last time I saw her was right after she had a baby. Her husband seemed like a very nice man, but, she was so busy with the baby, and I moved, we lost touch.

My relationship with my parents went from bad to worse as I grew older. My housework load kept going up, and I did my best, but my mother was never satisfied with me. There was also the fact that I never felt like it was ok to just be me. I refused to tell my parents anything, and they would occasionally badger me while getting answers like 'nowhere' and 'nothing.' I had learned that it was dangerous to share anything with them. I stopped going anywhere so they would leave me alone and not ask me questions, so I spent most of my teen years in my room reading books and daydreaming of a better life. That made my mother badger me about the fact that I never went anywhere. But that was easier to deal with than being grilled on where I was going because when I did go out I was usually walking aimlessly on my own. I knew that if I told them this it would just lead to more badgering so I did it when they weren't home. It got so bad that I finally asked the neighbor who had the extra key to our house for advice. She had children around my age and I was hoping she could help. She suggested I try compromising with my mother. If we could discuss the things that were bothering me and reach some middle ground things might get better. This seemed like sound advice to me so I tried it. The response I got was 'I am the mother, you are the daughter, you need to adjust to me, I am too old to change.' It sounded wrong to me but there was nothing I could do. My mother was seething, and trying any more would just make things worse. After that our key was in another neighbor's apartment, and I was forbidden to talk to the neighbor who had given me the advice.

Most Ulpanas were strictly boarding schools, but the one I went to was a mix. Girls who lived close enough were bused in every day, those who lived too far would board. The commuters were all in one class and the boarders were all in another. My high school class was very united. No one was deliberately shunned or bullied but there was definitely a hierarchy of sorts. I never belonged to any of the groups but I was tolerated on the fringes of any group I would choose to sit with. Even the most popular girls would tolerate me though they never made any effort to include me. I watched them put on plays and pull pranks on teachers. There was a code of silence with regard to the pranks, and I think part of the reason I was tolerated is that I kept my mouth shut along with everyone else. I wanted to be in the plays but was afraid to ask and they never invited me to participate even though I sat through all their rehearsals. This is very common with high masking autistic girls. There is a façade of fitting in, when in fact, we very rarely do. The façade is part of the mask. When I spoke I got ignored, and in our year book the few pictures I am in my face is partially cut off. So, while no one bullied me or told me to leave, I was invisible most of the time. To their credit the one time I accidentally pulled off a prank against a teacher they maintained the code of silence.

***

When I was about nine, one of my older brothers' friends had taught us how to make paper frogs. Ever since then whenever I have a blank piece of paper in my hands I am making paper frogs. I make a big frog, then use the leftover scrap to make a smaller one, and keep going until I can't make anymore and find another piece of paper. Sometime after my autism diagnosis I realized it was a form of stimming. That was another thing I was confused about when I first got the autism diagnosis. I didn't do any of the things autistics do like hand flapping, clapping, body rocking, or spinning. How could I be autistic if I didn't stim? Within a few days I realized that I do stim. I just do it in more subtle, and socially acceptable ways. One of my more common stims is wrapping a lock of hair around a finger and unwrapping it, over and over again. Sometimes I will braid a lock of hair, then undo it, and repeat multiple time. Whenever I am holding my keys I spin the key ring, and I will pick leaves off trees and bushes while out walking to fold and twist in my hand. If I am sitting on grass I pick at the grass, even the way I bite my finger while I'm driving is a stim. I could go on and on about the many ways I stim.

***

One day in high school, I must have been dealing with some overwhelm, and I started ripping sheets of paper out of my notebook and making frogs out of them. By the end of the first hour of that two hour class I had made about fifty frogs of various sizes. I was very proud of my work and put them on the teacher's desk to display. I had completely forgotten that the teachers nickname was froggy. I expected her to admire my handiwork but, of course, she got angry and demanded to know who had done it. The wall of silence was up. No matter what she threatened us with no one would speak. The whole class thought I had done it on purpose and they were delighted because they hated froggy. I decided to stay silent and not tell them it was unintentional. That day I was the class heroine, but it didn't last. The next day I was invisible again.

In the late seventies, when I was thirteen, my father started his own electronics company. The next summer when I was fourteen, and legally old enough to work, I spent the summer working for him soldering switches. Perach was working alongside me which made the tedious work bearable. The following summer half my class was working for my father. Israel had started broadcasting in color, but, for reasons related to equity they blocked the color, so, even if you had a color TV, you only saw black and white. My father came up with a device that would remove the block. The device became very popular very fast, and my father had to expand production quickly. We were a reliable, temporarily available, and cheap solution to his workforce needs. Some of the most popular girls were among those who worked for him, and this raised my stock with my classmates.

While I enjoyed the added respect, and modicum of acceptance I earned over that summer, and soldering boards was way more

22

interesting than the switches, I enjoyed my first summer working alone with Perach more. It was quieter, and I felt less disoriented. Back then my father had one full time employee who would check in on us every few hours and inspect our work. He was a young geeky engineer who would give us admonishing looks when we giggled. Perach and I would burst into roaring laughter every time he left the room.

The school felt it was important for us to connect to the land. This is actually quite common in Israel though I suspect we went on more trips than most. While in the bus we would sing old Israeli songs, that was my favorite part. While we were singing I felt a very rare sense of belonging. The popular girls chose the songs. Sometimes we would sing theme songs from children's shows like Kishkashta (similar to Barney but with a cactus puppet), and Hatzrif Shel Tamari Hanagar (Tamari the carpenters hut). I suppose that since these were educational shows the teachers didn't care. As long as we weren't being disruptive they left us alone, and I was glad to have that sense of belonging. I still remember the words to the songs we sang.

Once a month we would do a day trip to various sites, and once a year we would do a multi-day trip with lots of hiking. In ninth grade it was a two day trip and every year they added a day until in twelfth grade we did a 5 day trip to the Sinai. It was right before we gave it back to Egypt and it was a sort of farewell trip. We went to Mt. Sinai and Sharm El Sheikh, and other places I don't remember. I mostly remember lots of sand, and some fossils we weren't allowed to touch. Even though we were giving it back, we were expected to respect the land and not spoil it.

The trip I remember most vividly was our 11th grade trip to the Golan Heights. Specifically one section of one hike along Nahal Zavitan. It was the scariest hike I have ever been on, and I have done a lot of hiking, and a fair number of backpacking trips. There is a beautiful waterfall at the end of the hike, but, to get to it we had to navigate several hundred meters of jutting rocks moving sideways like crabs, about 20 meters (roughly 60 ft) above the river. It was a very rocky river, a fall would have most likely been fatal, and we had no safety gear. I was terrified! Halfway across I started crying. I have been scared on a lot of hiking and backpacking trips but only cried twice, and that was one of them. Looking back, I think I was in a meltdown both times. I tend to cry a lot when I am in meltdown, but thankfully I don't lose my motor skills. I did eventually make it, and thankfully the bus was waiting for us so we didn't have to go back the same way. I don't think I could have made it a second time.

***

You may be wondering what exactly do I mean by meltdown. Autistics deal with a lot of sensory issues because our brains don't filter out as much of the information coming in as allistic brains do. Because of all the additional information our brains constantly get we often get overwhelmed much more quickly than allistic people do, and autistic overwhelm is often more intense than allistic overwhelm. If we can back away from the trigger the overwhelm will pass after a short period. However, if the trigger persists we go into meltdown because our brains get pushed beyond their tolerance. Think of a pressure cooker. As long as the temperature under it isn't too high it can release enough pressure to maintain equilibrium. If you increase the heat too much it starts to whistle signaling it's building up more pressure than it can release (overwhelm). If you lower the temperature it will go back into equilibrium, but, if the pressure continues to build up it will explode (meltdown).

Contrary to what some people believe, once they start, autistic meltdowns cannot be controlled. An autistic person is not acting out when they are in meltdown. They are in an uncontrollable explosion from too much pressure. We cannot control our behavior during a meltdown any more than a pressure cooker can stop itself from exploding once it has reached that point. If you have an autistic person in your life who goes into meltdown too often you need to find out what the trigger is and remove, or, at the very least, minimize it. There may be more than one. Meltdowns are very hard on our system and can lead to shut down if they start occurring too often. Eventually, if they continue to happen often enough over a prolonged enough period, they can even lead to suicidality. How the meltdown looks and feels differs from autistic to autistic. They can even be different for the same autistic person depending on their mental state, and the meltdown trigger. I tend to cry a lot, or say things I shouldn't say, and if I have access to a device will start frantically sending emails about the thing that is triggering me to anyone I can think of who might be able to help me with it. Those emails tend to be very poorly

24

constructed. This can be disastrous in a professional setting, but I can't control it. The only way to prevent my meltdown behavior is to prevent the meltdown. But when you don't know you are autistic, you don't know how to explain to people why you do the things you do. You might know what's causing it, and ask to have the trigger removed, but more often than not you will get ignored. I would get dismissed as difficult demanding and disruptive whenever I tried to do that.

I used to think that when I was asked to do something, and I had questions about it, or thought it was the wrong thing to do, that I was being triggered by memories of the Holocaust where Nazi's later claimed they were just following orders. I knew I had to understand and be comfortable with what I was being asked to do, in order to follow through, and that was the most plausible explanation I could think of. While I do think it contributed, it is only part of what drives my need to understand, and agree with what I am being asked to do. The other part is my autism. Most autistics need to understand what and why we need to do something or we become overwhelmed, and can't do it. If I can't get an adequate explanation I often end up melting down. Have you ever woken up suddenly feeling like your brain is still half asleep? That sense of not being able to get it to do what you want it to do feels to me like I'm dragging my brain through thick mud when I try to get it to work. That's how I feel when I'm told to do something without understanding why. I can't get it to go there. When my mental health is bad it can feel like my brain is encased in cement and can't budge at all. My explanations of the Holocaust trigger would fall on deaf ears, and I am not sure if the autism explanation would be any better in today's society where people are expected to simply do as they are told and not ask questions. What knowing I am autistic would have given me is an explanation for my behavior. I spent 57 years unable to answer the question, "Why did you react like that."

Learning about autistic overwhelm, meltdowns and shut downs has given me so much insight into how I interact with the world. I have learned to recognize when I am in overwhelm, and to try and remove myself from the trigger before I go into meltdown. However, CPTSD triggers can send me from overwhelm to meltdown in seconds when my mental health is bad. Even though I understand what is happening, I sometimes have no time to try and mitigate the situation. How much stimulation I can handle, and how well I can regulate myself is directly linked to my mental health. The more stressed out, anxious, and/or shut down I am, the quicker I go into meltdown, the longer it lasts, and the more likely I am to go into a deep shut down. I am hoping that with my new found knowledge and understanding I will learn, over time, to regulate myself better. However, since there is no way to completely control the world around me, there is no way to completely prevent meltdowns from happening. All I can do is apologize and explain. Being able to do that is life changing.

***

The day trip I remember most vividly is when we went to Yad Vashem, Israels Holocaust Museum in Jerusalem. I remember it because there was a memorial plaque for the village of Mielitz where my father's father was from. The entire village was rounded up and taken to Auschwitz and gassed in one day. My grandfather had carried the heavy weight of survivals guilt the rest of his life. None of us know exactly what happened because he would never speak of it. We had a record of my great grandfather singing with his brother. They were both Rabbis and Cantors. Everything I know is the bits and pieces my father shared from the bits and pieces he picked up from his father growing up. There was a huge fight between my grandfather and great grandfather leading to my grandfather leaving and becoming an atheist. He took his wife and three children to what was then Palestine in 1934. My father was three years old at the time. I don't know for a fact why my grandfather chose that particular destination, but, I suspect it had something to do with the fact that my grandmother was born and raised in Jerusalem, in a place called Me'a She'arim (100 gates). My grandfather had been a scholar his entire life and had no marketable skills, so for the first few years he paved streets to make money to feed his wife and children, and keep a roof over their head. He eventually got a job working for Israels electric company, and that probably played a part in my father becoming an electrical engineer. My father loved telling us about his summers working for the electricity company climbing electrical poles to service them.

Growing up with my grandfather's story of leaving everything behind and surviving the greatest known tragedy in Jewish history had a profound effect on me. I took from it that convictions are more important than money (my great grandfather was very rich). I never cared too much about worldly possessions, the most important thing was to do what you think is right. While I lived in Israel I could fit all my possessions into my car, and it was a very small car. I became a little more materialistic after a few years back in the US, even going through a shopaholic period when I got my first permanent professional job, but never went too extravagant. When I bought my house I spent well below my means, and more towards my needs. 1100 square ft. is more than enough for one person in my opinion. I spent some of the money I saved on solar panels. I have wanted solar panel for as long as I can remember, and I finally have them. Reducing my carbon footprint has always been very important to me.

The final stage of the return of Sinai to Egypt happened when I was in twelfth grade. My parents were Zionists, my school was Zionist, and I was, and still am a Zionist, though not as radical as my parents or school were. Being a Zionist means supporting the right of Israel to exist as the national homeland of the Jewish people. My father voted for Kahana when he ran for Knesset, I was appalled. My hyper logical brain does not lend itself to radicalism of any kind. But I was very skeptical of the peace treaty in Egypt and felt the need to protest it. I went to live in an illegal settlement in the northern strip of the Sinai that was most populated and the last to be evacuated. The settlement was run by Gush Emunim. I wasn't opposed to the treaty in principle. I was willing to trade land for peace, but, there was a built in mistrust that I couldn't shake. I am happy to accept that I was wrong, and I paid a price for my actions.

When I decided to go to Sinai it was closed to anyone who wasn't a resident or a tourist. Since I wasn't a resident I would have to go as a tourist. I grabbed a novel in English, I mostly read in English anyways, my American passport, and boarded a bus without telling my parents where I was going. They were traveling on business, and had no idea what I was doing. When border patrol came aboard to check everyone's credentials I handed them my American passport as casually as I could and waited for an agonizing time while they looked from the photo to my face before handing it back and moving on. They never saw that it had been issued in Tel Aviv, or that I had no stamp for entering the country. I have never had a stamp from Israel on my American passport because I use my Israeli passport when I enter and leave Israel.

The other people at the settlement were very radical. I made friends with one girl from Jerusalem who would make statements like "we will never give up this land." I didn't say anything, but I didn't agree with her. I was willing to trade land for peace, I just didn't think we would get peace.

The day we were evacuated I was forcefully carried out by four soldiers, I made such a fuss that a reporter snapped a picture of me. We were loaded onto a bus where I did one of the most foolish things I have ever done in my life. We worked on the back window to pry it open and at one point when the bus slowed down and I thought it was stopping, I crawled out through the window. But the bus accelerated just as I was about to jump and I ended up hitting the road much harder than I anticipated, and in a bad position. I couldn't stand or walk, I had broken my kneecap. I spent six weeks in a no step cast, and another six weeks with the crutches partially stepping on my foot. My body became very asymmetrical and has never been quite the same again. I was supposed to do physical therapy after I was able to drop the crutches. I went once, learned how to slow down and walk more evenly without limping like a pirate on a short peg leg, and never went back. Since I could now walk I didn't see the point in going back.

A few weeks after the evacuation there was a knock on our door. It was the young French couple who lived next door to us, and the wife excitedly shoved a magazine into my hands "look, look." There in the centerfold of that month's *Paris Match* was a photograph of me being carried by four soldiers. I had my 15 minutes of fame. I have to admit that I love being able to tell people that I was once the centerfold of *Paris Match.*

Throughout high school I continued to perform poorly in most subjects. Though I had mastered the language by then, unless the subject interested me, I put little to no work into it. Some subjects like grammar were incomprehensible to me. My most hated subject was literature. The teacher was always asking What did the author mean?" That question angered me because, how am I supposed to know what the author meant? If you want to know what the author meant, ask the author! I can tell you what I think it means, but I can't tell you what the author thinks it means! The subjects I shined in were English, biology, physics and math.

As an English speaker I was exempt from English classes until eleventh grade when they arranged a teacher to work with us on the literature and grammar we would need to pass the Bagrut. The Bagrut is a nationwide standardized test you take. Bagrut grades are the only grades considered for university admissions. Up until then all the English lessons were free periods for me and the other English speakers. We now had two hours of literature and one hour of grammar a week. There were different levels for each subject, the more points you took the more difficult and comprehensive the exam would be. You needed a minimum of four points in English to be considered a high school graduate, six was the maximum and that was what we were expected to do as English speakers. I decided to take my English tests in eleventh grade.

I quickly realized that my chances of understanding the grammar were about zero so I appealed to the teacher. Because I couldn't find a reason to need grammar, I had a mental block with regard to it. We didn't actually need to know grammar in order to pass the six point test. The test was comprised of three parts. The first was an oral exam that I passed easily, thankfully I was confident enough to not get overwhelmed and go mute. I had spent the month leading up to the exam coaching all the twelfth graders. The second part consisted of filling the blanks in a sentence, answering questions on a short article that was read over the radio at a specific time during the test. It was called the unseen because no one could see it or hear it before that time. The third part was the literature test where we had to write a dialogue on one of the given subjects, and answer one literature question. I told the teacher I would prefer to focus on the literature rather than the grammar I wouldn't need and couldn't seem to comprehend. By that time, she had seen enough of my work to know I could pass without learning the grammar so she agreed. All my years of avid book reading was paying off. To this day I don't know exactly what a verb or noun are, or anything else about grammar. I did very well on the English exams scoring a 10 out of 10.

***

It is quite common for autistics to have gaps in their abilities. I always wondered why I had such a hard time with certain subjects, while others were so easy for me to grasp. The autism diagnosis explains that as well as my executive function gaps. My mental health plays a big part as well. The better my mental health is the better I am at mastering new tasks and making good executive function decisions. The more overwhelmed I am, the harder everything gets. When I am in shutdown, I barely function.

***

I majored in biology in high school so I put some effort into it and got a good grade. Physics was easy for me so I did well in that even though I didn't take any official Bagrut points for it. I struggled with chemistry in high school, but oddly, when I finally went to university it flipped. I suddenly found chemistry easy. Visualizations of the molecules interacting with each other would pop into my head during class, it all made sense to me. Physics, on the other hand, was suddenly a struggle. I have no explanation for this, but, I suspect it is related to autism.

Math was the biggest surprise. Until tenth grade I was failing math. I rarely paid attention to anything the teacher was saying and had no idea how to solve any of the problems. In eleventh grade we had to choose whether to do 3 points in math or 4. It seemed like a no brainer to me. I was failing math so I had no chance of passing a 4 point exam. Then I got the best piece of advice I have ever gotten in my life from my older brother. He told me to go for the 4 points because I could always drop down, but, if I went for the 3 points I would never be able to go up. This made sense to me so I listened and went for the 4 points.

The 4 point class was taught by a different teacher who came in twice a week just to teach the advanced math classes. He loved math, and his passion infected me, so I started paying attention. We started with trigonometry. On day one I couldn't solve a single problem, didn't even know what the difference was between a sin and a cos, or what they actually were. Within a month I was solving the hardest problems in the book. Then we moved on to algebra, and suddenly algebra was easy. Had I gone to the 3 point class I would have failed math because the same boring teachers who had taught me in ninth and tenth grade, taught those classes. Instead, I discovered a passion for math that has stayed with me. I even took calc III as an elective in college.

For the rest of the subjects I tested on, I barely scraped a passing grade. But it was enough for me to earn my high school diploma, and move on to new chapters of my life.

Chapter 5
Military Service

B efore we graduated the school took us to "declare religious exemption status" for the military. The military would be a bad influence on us, we needed to be protected. I went along with the rest of the class and signed the piece of paper. The school did encourage us to do national service instead, and most of us had something set up by the time we graduated. My intention was to do two years of national service. I wasn't shirking my responsibilities towards the country, just contributing in a different way.

Away from school and my parents, I was able to start thinking for myself. I started questioning a lot of things I had been indoctrinated to believe, and finally had the opportunity to start fully exploring who I was. About four months into my national service, I realized I was dissatisfied with what I was doing. Why did I deserve special treatment? I decided to rescind my declaration, and join the rest of the country. I was confident enough with my convictions to know that going to the military would not destroy my faith.

To my surprise, my father supported my decision to let myself get drafted. He had served during the war of independence as had his sisters, and saw no reason why I shouldn't serve. My mother on the other hand, reacted exactly the way I expected her to, with full hysterics. Having my father's support made it easier though there was no stopping the process after I rescinded my declaration. Within a month I got the draft letter. In March 1983 I joined the Israel Defense Forces. As I sat on the floor with the other new recruits listening to my new commanding officer talk about expectations, I thought to myself, "two years, I can do this, it can't be that bad." There were a lot of bad moments, a lot of fun moments, and a lot of in between. I have no regrets about my decision to allow myself to be drafted, I learned a lot and grew as a person from those experiences.

Basic training was a whirlwind of activity. We learned how to make our beds military style, how to care for our rifles, how to shoot our rifles, and how to march in formation. We also did guard duty, kitchen duty, late night spot inspections, and one long march. My knee hurt for days after that march, no one cared.

Sometime during basic training, we had the opportunity to donate blood. They encouraged us to do it by offering the rest of the day off and an extra day of leave next time we went home. At first I was told I couldn't donate because of my low weight. Throughout high school I had been chubby, but once I was out on my own getting more movement, and choosing when, and what to eat, I slimmed down to 105 lbs. which I thought looked ok on my 5' 3" frame. I have dealt with pretty severe body image issues my entire life. Even though I was rail thin for about twelve years there were other things I was critical about like how small my breasts are. Israeli men aren't as boob focused as American men are but it still bothered me. Even so, the thought of getting plastic surgery was, and still is, abhorrent to me. I've never even had a manicure.

I don't know why they changed their minds, maybe they needed more blood than they were getting, but, I was eventually allowed to donate blood. They had snacks for us to eat after the blood donation but I took one look at them and walked out. All the sandwiches had butter (maybe margarine). There was no way I could eat any of it. I should have asked for a sandwich without the butter but at that point I was still very uncomfortable asking for anything. I started getting light headed and went to lie down. This was acceptable since I had donated blood but I missed lunch. Two girls were nice enough to bring me a plate. Unfortunately, there was nothing on the plate I could eat. I managed to not pass out until dinner time, and found something to eat in the mess hall.

Food issues plagued me my entire service. I ended up stationed about fifty miles from home and would go back and forth every day so I could eat something at night. That was the only food I would eat all day. If the base was locked down, I wouldn't eat until we were out of lock down and I could go home to eat.

When I made my decision to rescind my declaration I knew that I would not be satisfied just being in the military. I had to do something I felt was really worthwhile, really contributing. Sitting in an office making coffee for a high-ranking officer wouldn't cut it. There was a stigma associated with having an office job while serving in the military, and I wanted to avoid that at all costs. I knew I couldn't be in a combat unit, after the war of independence women no longer in combat units. At some point that got reversed again because women started demanding the right to be in combat units. However, when I was serving, it was impossible. There were other things I could do that would be meaningful to me. I also wanted something that would "stretch" me, take me out of my comfort zone and pull me out of my shell. I was aware of how shy and timid I was and I wanted to use my military service to do something about it. The IDF tried to take our desires into consideration, but there were no guarantees. The last week of basic training recruiters from every branch were there talking to us and interviewing us for various positions. To my surprise and delight I got the position I wanted. It was the closest thing to a combat position a woman could be in. I was going to be an artillery instructor. It was a prestigious placement, and I was determined to do well.

Training to be an artillery instructor was like an extended basic training, but much more challenging, and way more fun. We had to experience everything the men we were going to be instructing experienced during their training, so things like stretcher marches, and some hazing happened. Everyone wanted me to be on the stretcher because I was so thin, but, two girls had leg injuries so they were on the stretchers. After about 15 minutes one of them fell out of her stretcher and I was relieved I wasn't on the stretcher. I wanted to do my part but the stretchers were heavy and I was struggling. One of the commanders replaced me and told me in no uncertain terms that I was not to try and carry the stretcher any more. They tried to get us to maintain silence. Getting thirty young women to maintain silence is like herding wild cats. The silence never lasted more than a few seconds, so we did a lot of running. Every time the silence was broken they made us run to keep us quiet.

I am a cat person, so when I found a kitten on base I took it in and named it after our lieutenant. A few days later we had our weekly inspection. I made sure everything was set up right but there was still a tiny kitten curled up asleep in the middle of my cot. I decided to take my chances. It was worth the look on our lieutenant's face when he found out the cat's name. I was allowed to keep it but not in the cabin. The kitten went to live in one of the female officers' offices, and I would visit him as often as I could. He was well on his way to becoming the base mascot. This was a good thing because I couldn't take him home. I already had a cat and she wouldn't tolerate having another cat in the house. I had tried a few times in the past.

The first time we saw the tanks we would be working with one of the commanders asked if anyone knew how to climb on to a tank. I had no idea but I saw what looked like a foothold and a place to grab onto so, to his astonishment, I walked up to one of the tanks and climbed on.

After the first two weeks we settled into a routine of having breakfast, then a morning inspection, then classes all day, then an evening debrief, then bed time. There was a lot to learn. When the men went through the training, after a short period, they were divided into groups based on their position in the tank. Drivers would take the driving related classes, gunners would take the gunning related classes, and loaders/communications would take the classes relevant to their duties. There was a little bit of overlap but for the most part they each had their own curriculum. We had to learn all of it.

Because this was something I had chosen and was interested in I did well in the classes, until we hit communications. For some reason I could not master those classes. I had no problem learning how an engine works, or how to use the guidance systems, but I hit a wall with communications. The radios made me uncomfortable. They were noisy, and I didn't like them, so barriers went up in my brain and I barely passed those classes. You may be thinking that firing a tank is way noisier than a radio, and you would be correct. But at this point we were just learning in the classroom, so I was fine with everything except the communications classes that were full of noisy radios. Until I got my autism diagnosis I never understood why I had done so poorly in communications.

About six weeks in we started doing hands on stuff. Most of it was fun, some of it was difficult, and some of it was an absolute nightmare. We didn't get to drive a nagmash (troops carrier), but we got to ride in one. We all agreed that it was the worst experience of the entire training. Yes, it was worse than having to run with a loaded stretcher. We were thrown around like rag dolls in that thing. I finally managed to somewhat brace myself by grabbing two handles and pushing my legs up against the wall across from me, but I was also dealing with motion sickness. I am very prone to motions sickness, and as a child my father always had to pull over in the middle of road trips because I had to vomit. Imagine how much worse a vehicle that was bouncing around on rough terrain was for me. That ride was a nightmare and we were all covered in bruises afterwards. None of us wanted to be in a nagmash ever again.

My motion sickness sensitivity is a sensory issue. Besides our five external senses there are some internal ones. One of them is called vestibular, and hypersensitivity to this sense makes a person more prone to motion sickness. To this day if I sit in the back seat of a car I get motion sickness. Another thing my vestibular hypersensitivity affects is my ability to climb ladders. I am ok on the first rung, I start to feel dizzy on the second rung, and I can't climb to the third rung. I always thought it was a fear of heights, now I know it's a sensory issue. What I still don't understand is why I can climb up the side of a mountain, but can't climb up to the third rung of a ladder.

The base was relatively small and there was a lot of training going on so they sent us with our tanks to another base to do our hands on with the tanks. Before we left we had to load shells into the tank's honeycomb. The shells were about 3-4 ft high, looked a lot like gigantic bullets, and weighed anywhere from 35-60 lbs. each, depending on the type of shell. The shells were packed in crates, two shells to a crate and each shell was in its own sleeve. The tricky part was getting the shell out of the sleeve. One of the commanders demonstrated how to do it, making it look easy. But, for a 5'3" 105lb young woman it wasn't that easy. I couldn't pull the shells up out of the sleeves the way he demonstrated, so I had to figure something else out. I started walking backwards, slowly the shell started peeling out of the sleeve until enough was exposed for me to prop it with one leg while I got my arms around it, and pulled it out. I proudly walked over to a tank and handed it to one of my classmates who was on the conveyer belt to the tank honeycomb, where shells were stored. As I walked back to get another shell I noticed a busload of soldiers parked across the street. They were all laughing and pointing at me and I realized just how ridiculous I must have looked going through all those maneuvers to get the shell out of the sleeve. I didn't care. Besides being used to being laughed at, I was proud of finding a solution that worked. It took me three times longer to pull out a shell than anyone else, but I was doing it. So I just waved and laughed with them.

We were lodged in a remote part of the base with virtually no amenities. The bathrooms were holes in the ground, and there were no showers. To make matters worse we had to wear the tank overalls while we were there which meant practically stripping down completely every time we needed to go. I hated it. Then something went wrong with the tanks and they had to be fixed before we could use them.

Normally the tank crew would fix anything that was wrong with a tank, but, while they taught us the basics of tank maintenance, we never learned enough to actually fix anything, so we had a crew of mechanics that were responsible for our tanks. This meant that for the next day or two there was nothing for us to do. I had some books with me so reading seemed like the thing to do and I did. However, the class queen decided she wanted to sunbathe, stripped down to her underwear dragged her mattress (a piece of foam with a vinyl casing) and plopped down outside like she was on a towel at the beach to sunbathe. After that the rest of the class joined her so I dragged my mattress out too. I wasn't comfortable stripping down to my underwear but put on a t-shirt and shorts, and read outside in the blazing sun.

Within a few hours our commanders showed up and told us to get ready for a spot inspection. I can only imagine what it was like for them to find us sunbathing practically naked, but they had no choice but to rally us into action. Our base commander had driven down for a meeting and wanted to see us. We had twenty minutes to be ready for inspection. We were expected to be in our tank coveralls, hair neatly tied back and our bunks had to be ready for inspection as well. There was a crazy flurry of activity but we were ready on time. It was hard to keep a straight face during the inspection as I thought about what could have happened if the base commander had just driven over without any warning.

The next day our tanks were ready, and they asked for four volunteers. My brother had warned me to never volunteer for anything while in the military, but this time, I chose to ignore him, and immediately stepped forward. The four of us who volunteered got to ride in the tanks to the shooting range while the others rode in the bus. Tanks were not allowed to be moved without at least two people in them. I was so happy I had volunteered. Because of the technical problems we weren't able to get as much hands on as planned, but, we each got to experience every aspect of being a tank crew member. Driving was fun, you feel invincible in a tank, but my tank commander chose to not close the hatch and sand was blowing in my face.

37

I kept yelling, "I can't see anything."

And he kept yelling back, "Don't worry I can see."

But I was in a panic. Later I had to have sand removed from my eyes. Between being a hyper sensitive autistic and wearing contact lenses the sand in my eyes was excruciatingly painful, and I could tell that the tank commander was not happy about me complaining. Once again I got labeled difficult and demanding because I stood up for my needs.

Firing the tank main canon was a bit anticlimactic. We were so far from the target that I couldn't see if I had hit anything. Once again I had to rely on the tank commander who, using binoculars, gave me corrections and on my fourth try I hit the target. While I was happy about hitting the target I wished I could have seen more. Loading was a nightmare for me and I needed help pulling down the hammer. Nowadays they are automated but back then we had to do it manually. The hammer weighed 20 lbs. more than I did, and the spring holding it was very powerful to be able to hold it up. The instructor who taught that class told us it was a matter of technique rather than strength. Since she was even smaller than me and was able to do it I believed her, but, I was never able to master the technique. Every time I tried I ended up swinging on the handle and the hammer had not budged. Then, just to make things harder, my tank commander told me to put the last shell "up there" pointing to the highest point in the honeycomb. It was over a foot over my head, and I tried but there was no way I could lift a shell that high. I was barely able to get it into the lowest row. He hadn't asked the soldier who loaded for me to do that so it's possible he was getting back at me for complaining about my eyes the previous day.

The best part of weapons firing was the mounted automatic. Our lieutenant was in charge of that part. When it was my turn he pointed at a point a few feet from the tank and said, "enemy infantry there, get them."

I aimed and fired. It was way more fun than I could have imagined. Then to top it off the lieutenant turned to me and said, "Do you have one at home? Have you been practicing? That was amazing!"

Maybe he said that to everyone, but, it made all the misery of the trip worthwhile.

The last part of our training was conducted off base at a recreational facility in Netanya, Beit Goldmintz. We were there to hone our instruction skills. We were given tips about certain words to refrain from because they could have sexual connotations. We were taught how much to move around, proper eye contact when teaching, and many more things. This might be why I handle eye contact so well compared to other autistics. They also had us do some role playing so we could practice how to handle men who got fresh with us. We took turns pretending to be a fresh guy, and responding to the heckling. When it was my turn to play a guy I was assigned the role of a reserve soldier. This would be someone much older, more experienced, and harder to handle because he would typically be back in the military for no more than 30 days, unless there was an active war. I threw myself into the part. I had taken a few acting classes one summer and drew from everything I had learned.

"Hey honey, can I get your number," I boomed in the lowest register I could muster and with as much swagger as I could give. The instructor's eyes popped open and we all started laughing hysterically.

Drawing from every obnoxious comment guys had thrown at me over the years, I continued to throw out "pearls" being as obnoxious as I could, and had everyone rolling with laughter the whole time. One of the reasons it was so funny is that I was normally so quiet and reserved. Through that experience I realized that making people laugh was fun, and that I was apparently good at it. Making people laugh would become my go to in social situations. Since I was weird and awkward this seemed like a good way to ease the tension my weirdness created. Having people laugh with me, and even at me was significantly better than being invisible. I memorized a few jokes, put together a bunch of one liners, and quips, and would strive to make people laugh as often as I could. Even my therapist has commented on how fun my quirky sense of humor is. But I had to work at it. It took me years to understand certain jokes. Many autistics never master humor. But with dedication and time I succeeded. I even have a little standup comedy routine I tell people who will listen.

While we were at the facility honing our teaching skills, there was an officers course at a nearby facility, Beit Feldman, working on, well, I have no idea, but they were there working on something. The facilities were less than a mile apart, and one of the girls in my course knew one of the guys in the officers course. We got invited to kumzitz on the beach. Back then this was a very common form of getting together. You sit by a bonfire, sing songs, and roast things to eat. The activity had been popular long before the state was founded. There are a lot of old Israeli songs about sitting around a campfire singing songs.

The day of the kumzitz I received my Scientific American. At that time this was a difficult read for me, so I decided I would skip the kumzitz in order to read the magazine in peaceful silence while everyone was gone. I have never been able to focus with background noise, not even music. The girls checked in on me before leaving, but I assured them I was happy staying behind reading my magazine. There was a cell on the cover and it looked to be an interesting read. As soon as they were gone I delved into the main article on the newly discovered cell cytoskeleton. About half an hour later four soldiers from the officers course showed up.

"We came to get everyone," one of them said.

I told them the girls had left about half an hour ago and they were crestfallen. "We told everyone we would bring the girls. What about you?"

I explained that I had deliberately stayed behind to read, but they wouldn't accept it. They begged me until I agreed to go with them.

"We should go down to the beach and make sure they aren't lost," one of the soldiers said.

The kumzitz had been moved from the beach to a grassy area next to the facility they were staying at. Their concern made sense to me, and we headed to the beach. As we walked down the path to the beach in the dusky light two of our tank commanders were walking up.

"Evening swim?" I asked them.

"Yes," one of them replied. "And where are you going?"

"Oh, I'm going to a kumzitz."

He gave me a strange look and said, "Kumzitz huh?"

"Yes," I replied, puzzled by the strange look he was giving me.

We continued down to the beach, and they continued back up to the facility.

As we walked along the beach my nerves settled from that strange interaction, and I started looking around. Then it hit me. Sand, sand, sea, cliffs, and I am alone with four men. I had a moment of panic then realized, I'm a soldier and they are in officers' course. If they touched me against my will their careers would be over. Not just in the military, but their entire lives. I was safe. A few moments later I realized what the tank commander had been insinuating and to diffuse my discomfort I started to laugh out loud.

"What?" they all wanted to know.

I explained to them what I had figured out, and we all had a good laugh. I was at ease again, and we kept walking.

After a few more minutes we arrived at a point below their facility. It was completely dark by then and we could see the light from the fire and heard everyone singing.

"I don't want to go all the way around," one of the soldiers said. "Let's climb up."

Fear struck me, along with my mutism. They quickly organized themselves, two ahead of me to find the best path, and two behind me to make sure I was safe. As we started climbing I kept saying to myself, "Just focus, one foot at a time, one arm at a time, and don't look down," over and over like a mantra. I was shaking like a leaf in the wind but the mantra kept me focused and other than the last few feet where one of them offered me the butt of his rifle and pulled me up because it was a particularly difficult section, I climbed the whole thing myself, and didn't have a meltdown.

As soon as I was on solid ground I collapsed and found my voice. I told them about my fear of heights and how scared I was.

"Why didn't you tell us, we would have gone around," they told me.

I had no answer. I didn't even realize at that time that I had a speaking problem. It wouldn't be until almost forty years later, close to my autism diagnosis, that I would realize I had this problem.

I told the girls about my little run in with the tank commanders and they roared with laughter.

"Of all of us, you," one of them said.

They all knew I was still a virgin, I was the only one. I assumed at the time that this was what she was referring to, but now I wonder, was there some other meaning behind that comment? I don't remember feeling put down by it, so it's more than likely that my first conclusion was correct. Most of the time I would pick up on "something" when a comment meant to be a putdown was made at me, though I had no idea what that something was.

Chapter 6
Avi

Even though I had done well on almost everything I ended up
with the subject no one wanted. Defense against WMD's. It
was considered a joke. The movie "Day After" had just been
released and everyone assumed they would be dead if WMD's were
deployed. It would be hard to get anyone to take the subject seriously.
I was demoralized but determined to do well. This was one of the
overlap classes, I would be instructing everyone.

In order to teach the class, I would need more training. My new
commanding officer told me where to go to sign up for the course. I
would need, a three week course on defense against WMD's. I found
the office and spoke with a soldier who was moving piles of books. I
would ask a question, he would answer it, then grab a stack of books
and disappear for a minute. When he came back I would ask another
question, he would answer, grab some books, and disappear for a
minute.

After a while he stopped, gave me a long hard look and said, "Will
you marry me?"

This was the first time a man had ever paid any attention to me.
Besides that, he had the most beautiful dark blue eyes I had ever seen.
I said yes and he looked very pleased with himself. I later learned that
his mother had just chided him on not taking any of his relationships
seriously and that if he continued like this he would never get married
and have children. So when he saw me, and liked what he saw, he
decided to just ask me to marry him. From my perspective, my parents
had gotten engaged after dating for three weeks, and I had heard
countless other stories of people meeting, falling in love, and marrying
quickly. Both sets of my grandparents had been in arranged marriages
and didn't know each other when they married. It wasn't that
uncommon in Israel for things to go very fast. The entire country was
like a ticking time bomb, and no one had time to wait for years to
establish a relationship. Men knew they could be at war anytime and

die, so the sooner they had kids the better.

The course started the following week and I was the only woman in it. They had to arrange special quarters for me. There were women's barracks, but they didn't want to put me there because I would be having very early morning activities, and they didn't want all the women to be inconvenienced by my schedule. So I was placed in an old abandoned building by myself. That first day Avi (my fiancé) told me to be ready at seven PM. He knew we wouldn't have any activities later than that, and it would be dark. Because I was in training I wasn't allowed to leave the base. He snuck me out through a hole in the fence and took me home to meet his mother and younger sister. For the rest of the course he would sneak me out several nights a week and take me home for a few hours. The rest of the courses commanders knew what we were doing, but they said nothing. We never got caught.

It was a grueling training, but, being the only woman, I cruised through it. They couldn't give me guard duty because women could only do guard duty in pairs, and none of the women on base did guard duty. There was kitchen duty, but I never got assigned. One of the trainees was in charge of the schedule and he never scheduled me for kitchen duty. I had to be outside the men's quarters at 5 am every morning for morning inspection. After the inspection we would go on a run and do calisthenics with a gas mask on. Well, the men would run and do calisthenics with a gas mask on. I would walk over and by the time I got there they would be done and we would all walk back together. They knew I was engaged to Avi but they didn't care. Most of them were reserve soldiers, and were married with children. They were happy just having a woman around.

I showed up for inspection one morning and everyone was busy cleaning their rifles. They had been tipped off that rifles would be inspected that day. I barely saw my rifle. I would pick it up from Avi's quarters every morning for inspection and give it back to him after we were done. I figured it wouldn't hurt to clean the barrel so I asked one of my classmates if I could borrow his choter (a long thin rod used to clean gun barrels).

He held out a hand and said, "Here, give it to me, I'll clean it for you."

He took my rifle apart and cleaned the entire rifle for me. The men in my class would do anything for me, and all they wanted in return was a smile. I didn't understand it, but I wasn't going to complain.

43

During inspection the course lieutenant started randomly inspecting people's rifles. When he got to me, he paused then said, "Soldier, is your rifle clean?"

"Yes sir," I responded.

He looked at me suspiciously. He knew Avi had my rifle all the time. He asked to see it, peered into the barrel, and I could tell, he was surprised it was clean. My classmates were smiling and winking at me. The lieutenant handed back the rifle, glared at me and said, "Soldier why didn't you shave this morning?"

I knew he had to be joking but I had no idea how to respond. Then he started laughing and we all laughed with him.

The last week was a field exercise. We would be living in tents, sleeping on the floor with sleeping bags, holes in the ground for toilets, and no showers. But this time, it would be for six days, and we weren't on a base, we were in the wilderness. I often struggle with showering. I enjoy the actual shower, but getting in, getting out, and most of all drying off have always been difficult for me. Taking a shower takes me three times as long as it should because I am so exhausted when I am done that I have to lie down for up to 30 minutes before I can put my clothes on. I never looked forward to a shower as much as I did during those six days in the field.

Day one we got everything set up. I was the only girl there, but, because we were in the field there were no special quarters for me. I had to sleep in the big tent with all the guys. There were groups from every military discipline there to participate in the exercise, hundreds of men. I never felt so self-conscious before. Guys were hitting on me at every turn and Avi was no help. He thought it was funny. He told me to just tell them off but I had no idea how to respond to these guys. I just wanted to run away. Little did I know, was that much worse was coming.

Day two we got fitted for our gas masks and did the tear gas tent drill. In order to test the seal on the mask they used an inert but pungent tester, you would put on a mask and try to smell it. If you couldn't smell it you were good to go with that mask. When my turn came I tried every size mask, but no matter how much I tightened the straps I could still smell the tester. The course lieutenant got irritated, thought I was being difficult, and trying to get out of doing the exercise. So he ordered me to pick a mask and get in line for the tear gas tent. I had no choice but to do it. I took the smallest mask and got in line. In the gas tent exercise, you walk to the middle of the tent where you had to take off your mask then give your name, rank, and serial number before you could run out. It took a few minutes to get to the middle because there were so many people ahead of you, and I was gagging on the tear gas from the moment I stepped in.

***

What I understand now is that I can smell things at a much lower concentration than allistic people can, and it affects me at that lower concentration. Even if a gas mask fit me within allistic parameters, I would still be affected, so it's possible one of them did fit within those parameters. Years later my workplace would get the building we were working in re-carpeted. They moved us to another building for a week while the work was being done and then a few more days to let the building air out. We went back in after the air was tested and deemed safe. Everyone else was fine, I was choking. The only way I could sit at my desk was with the window wide open and three fans running to keep the fresh air in my face. It was February and no one was happy about my open window. The minute I stepped away from my desk I started choking again. My bosses did take me seriously, and they checked, and double checked, but could find no reason for me to be having the problems I was having. Not knowing I am autistic, I couldn't explain it to them. I was allowed to keep my open window, and the fans, but got a lot of dirty looks, and the guy in the cubicle next to me was furious.

***

The tear gas tent was a nightmare but things were about to get way worse. The next day we started the field exercise. We were divided into two groups and did a simulated battle scenario. In order to create a chemical attack scenario, they had a crop duster fly over and dump tear gas on us from the sky. Now I was stuck in it with no way to run out. It covered several square miles. They repeated this for three days while we played out different battle scenarios. I have no idea what the scenarios were, I was too busy trying to stay conscious. I wanted to pass out but I was afraid I would die from exposure if I did. Avi told me to climb to the highest spot I could find where the chemical concentration would be the lowest, but he couldn't stay with me because of his command position.

I got my certificate and went back to my own base. Next I learned the script for the class I was supposed to teach and was ready to start being an instructor. The only soldiers on base at the time was a tank commanders course, so I had to teach my first class to a group of soldiers who knew more about what I was teaching than I did. The Q&A section was embarrassing and I vowed to become an expert on the subject.

When an autistic takes an interest in a subject they often become obsessive about it. At least once a month I would go back to the base where I did my defense against WMD's course and get material from them. As I learned more and more on the subject I started making changes to the curriculum. With my commanding officer's permission, I eventually did a complete overhaul of the material, and class structures. When I started teaching there was one class that was taught to new soldiers, tank commander courses, and officer courses. I created completely new classes with completely different information for the tank commander's class, and the officers class. There were protocols that had to be followed in the event of a WMD attack and they each needed to learn the protocols for their level of command. I also expanded all the classes to include some biological and atomic incidents.

It took a while but I slowly learned how to control my class. What worked best for me was humor. As long as I could get them to laugh things went smoothly. Then by the time I had overhauled the curriculum I was worn out. You can't just take a vacation in the military, which is what I needed, so I switched to a less demanding position. For my last few months of service, I worked as a night shift switchboard operator.

My biggest problem on base, even worse than the food, was cigarettes. When I was in the army there were no rules about smoking and I am hyper sensitive to cigarette smoke. I can smell it when no one else can, and it makes me sick. But there was nothing I could do about it. Most people smoked, and no matter how much I tried to wriggle my way into a position where it wasn't blowing in my face during meetings, I couldn't escape it. Everyone kept trying to convince me to just "join the club" but I don't have the words to describe how repulsed the thought of smoking a cigarette, or anything else, is to me. I am curious about marijuana, and for years I wished I could try it, just once to see what it was like, but there was no way I could ever smoke a joint. At this point I am no longer interested in even trying. I seem to be getting more and more sensitive as I get older and I don't think it would agree with me.

The base I was on was semi closed. Once I was out of training and certified as an instructor I was able to go home every night unless the based closed. It would take me over an hour to travel each way but I needed to eat, and the food on base was inedible for me. The base commander would close the base every so often for a mandatory meeting we all had to go to. Besides not being able to eat for two days, I had to deal with a meeting that lasted several hours with hundreds of people smoking in the auditorium. I would slowly sink down further and further towards the floor trying to find a gasp of clean air while everyone around me mindlessly blew smoke. I would be sick for hours after those meetings.

My relationship with Avi continued for several months until his mother started asking us where we were planning to live and how we were planning on supporting ourselves. She thought we were too young to get married and wanted us to wait until we finished university. Avi became depressed, and I didn't know how to handle the change in him. I didn't know it at the time, but, I was having daily meltdowns over our relationship. My parents had given me no relationship skills, and I was confused and hurt by his behavior. I finally ended the relationship. I was miserable but didn't know what else to do. I thought it was what he wanted. I wish I had been more patient. I ran into him about a year later. I desperately wanted to ask him if he wanted to get back together but couldn't get the words out of my mouth. I kept hoping he would say something to indicate how he felt about me but he said nothing though I had the feeling he was waiting for me to say something. I saw Avi one more time, at Ben Gurion Airport as I was going through security. He was working in airport security, standing about 50 ft away from me talking to some of his coworkers. I desperately wanted to go over and talk to him, but had no idea what to say. I doubted he would even remember me. After all, he was my first everything, but I was just another girl in a long string of girls for him. Even though I had already dated several more men, and had two more proposals that I turned down, I was still totally hung up on Avi. I have never seen him since. That entire experience with Avi had a profound effect on me. I realize now that after our breakup I closed myself off not wanting to get hurt again. I dated dozens of men, got several proposals, and turned them all down. I didn't realize it at the time, but, I still wanted Avi, and only Avi. Looking back, every guy I dated, every guy I felt any sort of attraction to over the rest of my life, bore a resemblance to him.

Chapter 7
Horses

After I got out of the army I didn't really know what I wanted to do with my life. My parents wanted me to go to university but I didn't see the point. Nothing interested me enough, and I knew that without the interest I wouldn't do well. I drifted from job to job and relationship to relationship. Nothing ever lasted long. I always managed to upset people at work. I would start with a lot of enthusiasm, be pushing myself as hard as I could. Over time I would deflate like a tire with a nail in it until I started having meltdowns which would lead to my employer no longer wanting me around. Not knowing about my autism, not having any explanations, or even awareness of what was happening kept getting me fired. Every once in a while I would have a job I loved, and things would be going well, and the place would shut down.

Over the years I did many things, reservations and ticketing for airlines, horseback riding instructor, agriculture worker, waitress, house cleaning, and nanny. One of the reasons I had so few possessions is that I moved so much. I never seemed to fit in anywhere, so I kept moving trying to find my place in the world.

The more a guy was into me the more quickly I lost interest in him. I was at war with myself. Part of me wanted to get married and have kids, and part of me was terrified of getting hurt again, and pushed away anyone who got too close. I finally decided I didn't want kids. Not because I don't like children, but, because there are already so many children in need. I thought that if I was ever able to care for a child I would adopt one of those kids. After I made that decision I started pushing men away even more.

When I was twenty four, my father's business went bankrupt and my parents moved back to the United States. I decided to stay in Israel. Even though we had been back for visits over the years, Israel was home and I couldn't bear the thought of leaving. It was also an opportunity to distance myself from my parents and be free to figure out who I really am. One of the first things I figured out is that I don't believe in God. Over the years I would waver back and forth between being a total atheist and an agnostic who accepts that it's possible there is some powerful entity out there. But the god described in the main religions is a complete farce to me. God didn't create us, we created God.

The day I gave up on religion was a Saturday, the Sabbath. I stared at a light switch for a while and finally said, "if you exist God, strike me down" and flipped the switch. Nothing happened. I defiantly flipped the switch a few more times before I was fully convinced I wouldn't be struck down for turning on a light on the Sabbath. After that I started looking for ways to defy the rules. I ate a pork chop sandwich at a friend's house, rode in a car on Sabbath, and started wearing pants and t-shirts. My mother never let me wear t-shirts because they were too immodest, and girls only wore skirts. That first Yom Kippur I defiantly made a feast with some friends, and we had as many non-kosher dishes as we could.

I no longer do anything out of defiance, I even fast on Yom Kippur to feel part of the Jewish community, but, I am still agnostic/atheist. I do know that, if I ever found faith again, I would go back to Judaism. I once told a rabbi that I have my doubts about God, but, that if God does exist I am in the right religion. She responded with, "That's OK, God can handle it."

It's highly unlikely that I will ever be religious again. To me Judaism is my culture, and it's very important to me, though I didn't realize how much until I was almost forty.

Animals have always been a very important part of my life. Around the time I was forbidden from visiting our neighbor with the dog, a cat showed up at our house. The cat was black and white so we named it Marble, started feeding it, and it stuck around for a few weeks, then disappeared. I was so heartbroken that my parents got a new kitten. We named her Buffy and I poured all my love into her. We gave her to some distant cousins who lived in California when we moved to Israel, I never saw her again, but I do know that she lived to the ripe old age of eighteen.

My mother didn't want any other animals. I kept finding strays and trying to bring them home to no avail. When Perach's cat had kittens I took one home. My mother didn't want it in the house so I had to put it in the garbage chute room, caring for, and playing with it next to the smelly garbage. The kitten got sick and my mother grudgingly agreed to take it to a vet who said it was too sick to be saved and put it down. I was heartbroken.

The vet started showing up at our house every week. He was going to work in the US, and arranged to take English lessons with my mother. He must have seen how unhappy I was because one day he called and told me over the phone to come downstairs. When I got downstairs he handed me a box. I peeked inside and there was an orange, black and white kitten.

"It's for you," he said.

I rushed upstairs with my new kitten wondering if I would have to keep this one in the garbage chute room as well. My mother let me keep her in the house with the understanding that when we weren't home it would be outside. She didn't want a litter box. I think she was concerned with how the vet would react if we kept the kitten in the garbage chute room. By the time he left for the U.S. Cali was entrenched in our apartment. I was no longer alone when I read my books and daydreamed, Cali was always there with me.

My younger brother would try to claim Cali as his own, but she was always with me, and slept in my bed. My mother once commented that when I was away for more than a day, she would park herself at the threshold of my room and wait for me, ignoring everyone else. She was MY cat.

During the two months between ending my national service and conscription I worked for my father and used the money to take horseback riding lessons at a local stable. I had always been obsessed with horses but my parents didn't think it was appropriate for a "nice Jewish girl." So I would sneak off and use the money I made working for my father during summers to go to a rental stable in Netanya and ride as much as the money would let me. More than anything I wanted my own horse but it seemed impossible.

When I got out of the army I went to work in small riding school run by an eccentric. He didn't pay me but gave me free lessons every day. After a few months I managed to get into an argument with him and left. I don't remember what the argument was about. For a while I went to work for El Al as a reservations clerk, then United Airlines as a ticketing and reservations clerk, then Pan Am. I was very good at reservations and ticketing. I knew all the prices by heart, I could multi task and be working with someone on the phone while making a ticket for someone else. During the spring and summer things would get so hectic I wouldn't even have time to drink a cup of coffee if someone was nice enough to bring me one. I loved the high activity. After work I would go riding. I had found a stable where private horses were boarded and would ride other people's horses. I mainly rode for a man who would buy and sell horses for a living, so every few weeks I had a different horse to ride.

Soon after my parents left for the US, I bought my first horse. He was a stallion, with a lot of Arabian blood in him, quite small, only 15 hands, not much to look at, but all heart and shock proof. I could ride him on a long rein along a busy highway, or next to a train, and he would barely twitch his ears. The only time he became feisty was when I would take him on longer rides, at least two hours and let him canter along the beach for miles. He was an endurance horse. The more he ran, the more energy he had. But I wanted to do dressage. To quote a British trainer I took some lessons with "He doesn't look like much, and will never have an impressive stride, but he has the head and heart to be able to do a Grand Prix." Six months after the trainer made that comment he was stolen, and I never found him.

I was heartbroken over his loss and poured even more love into Cali while I worked through the loss. I knew I would get another horse, went around looking at lots of horses but none of them were the one. One day I went to check out a small stable that had just changed ownership and I saw him. I had dreamt about him the night before, and there he was. A scrawny undeveloped 3 year old who had been raced once and won. He was scrawny because they were afraid of him. He was so high strung they kept him half starved to try and control him. I had a vet check him out and bought him. He had virtually no training, and kept trying to bite me when I led him home. The next day I saddled him up to go for a ride and as soon as I was in the saddle he tried to take off. I spent the next two days teaching him to stay in a walk. When I was able to ride him with a long rein and stay in a walk I introduced trotting. Getting him to stay in a trot was much more challenging, and it took two weeks. Next I worked on keeping him in a controlled canter for a few weeks, then I took him to an arena. He kept trying to jump out of the arena, and every time a horse in a neighboring arena would jump, he would leap in the air. I booked a lesson with a trainer, he asked me to ride for a few minutes to see what we were working with and kept saying, "Oh, he's green, he's very,

very green." I had my work cut out for me.

I went to the U.S. for the next Passover. My mother wanted to have the whole family together and I foolishly let myself get hooked in. I sent my horse to stay with a friend and my landlords took care of my cat. I kept my horse in a small DIY stable where all they provided was a stall, so I couldn't just leave him there. My landlords hated cats when I first moved in. I was renting a small renovated egg storage building on their property. But, they learned to love Cali. In fact, they loved her so much that by the time I left they had two cats of their own.

When I got back my friend told me in no uncertain terms that I was wasting my time trying to do dressage with Magic, he was a jumper. I was still too spooked from a jumping accident I had with Strider that had ruptured my disc, so I continued to work with him on dressage even though I knew she was right. Magic wanted to jump so much that when I was in the dressage arena, he would leap in air every time another horse in a nearby arena would go over a jump. It would take me a few more years to start jumping with him.

My dressage years with Magic were difficult, but I learned so much from them. My first horse, Strider, was a pleaser. He was constantly trying to figure out what I wanted from him, and would then give it to me. Magic on the other hand was "difficult." I couldn't get him to do anything. I was getting very frustrated with him and was starting to think I would never be able to do any dressage with him when I finally realized what his deal was. Magic was not a thinker, he was a reactor. The first time I got a request right he performed. I had to get it right to get what I wanted from him. I never got very far with him in dressage but I learned a whole lot about what I was doing wrong because, every time I got it right, he performed beautifully.

Eventually, I started jumping with Magic, taking baby steps because I was still very afraid. Besides of my injury I had a fear of heights, or maybe it was the vestibular sensory issues, possibly both. When it came to jumping, Magic was all heart. He would jump anything for me. My fears and lack of money to pay trainers were the only things that prevented me from making him a top jumper. He also settled down a little after I started jumping with him. He was still spooky and jittery, but much less than before. A trainer got up on him once and gave me what I consider a compliment. He said Magic was very soft and responsive, that I hadn't done much with him but I hadn't

53

ruined him like so many amateurs do with their horses. I knew exactly what he meant because from time to time I would let someone else ride Magic for a while and he would become less responsive. I would end the agreement, and it would take a few months to get him back to where he was when I was the only one riding him.

Soon after resuming jumping with Magic the Israel Horseback Riding Federation was looking for show jumping judges. I decided to take the initial test. I passed along with several others, and started my internship. Being an obsessive autistic, I was the first one to finish my internship, and notified the head judge I was ready for my final test. There was no doubt in my mind that I could pass the test. Two days before the test I got call from the biggest stable in the country. They had a training competition scheduled for that weekend and could not find a judge. My test was scheduled for the day before the competition, and they asked if I could preside over the competition. The head judge had told them I was certain to pass. Fear struck me... *"What if I didn't pass?"*

Suddenly I felt pressured because so many people would be counting on me, and know if I failed. I told them I would do it if I passed the test. They told me they were sure I would, but the more people said this to me the more stressed I became. It occurred to me that maybe I should study for the test now, but I couldn't focus enough to do it. I would have to rely on the knowledge I already had.

Thankfully, despite my nerves I passed the test. In many ways being a judge helped me feel more accepted because I was suddenly needed. But it also created conflict. Everyone wanted special treatment and I struggle with that concept. Rules exist to level the playing field. It made no sense to me to give some people an advantage by bending the rules for them. There is nothing more difficult to deal with than the parent of a competing child who won't accept their child's results.

Chapter 8
Cats

Autistics tend to be very good with animals. Animals are much less complicated to understand and deal with than people. It is quite common for a pet to be the sole friend of an autistic.

When Cali died, at age 19, I took in a pair of young street cats I had known since they were kittens. I could write an entire book on those cats, but, I doubt anyone would want to read that book, so I will only share the highlights to demonstrate the bond we had. My cats were the only living beings who loved me unconditionally my entire life. The first few days were very difficult, they were afraid of every noise in the apartment, but over time they adapted. I named them Tziki and Miri. Miri was already pregnant so I knew kittens were on the way. I decided to get the Tziki neutered right away to avoid problems down the road.

I came home from work one day and there was Miri with a black and white kitten that looked a lot like her. I sat with them for a few minutes then went to cook dinner. Miri followed me, placed the kitten at my feet and cried. I went back to the couch, and sat with them for a few more minutes, then tried to get my dinner going again, and Miri brought the kitten back to me and cried. I wondered if she didn't know how to care for it. This happened a few more times before I started wondering where the other kittens were. Cats generally have more than one kitten. I sat with her again and this time tried to feel for more kittens. I felt some movement so I called a vet to find out what the longest time between kittens normally was. It had been over an hour since I got home. The vet suggested bringing her over and sent his assistance with a carrier. The moment his assistant walked in the door Miri became a wild animal hissing and spitting. I asked the assistant to step outside. She stood outside with the door cracked open watching. Miri settled down the moment she was out of sight and I started talking to her and trying to coax her into the carrier. When I put the kitten inside the carrier she walked right in. I quickly retrieved the kitten, shut the cage door and let the assistant back in.

We took Miri and her kitten to the vet where he tried to examine Miri but she was so ferocious that even with her in the cage, using protective gloves they couldn't control her (she was a tiny cat, Tziki was twice her size, but she could be as ferocious as a tiger). The vet had to sedate her to examine her. There were two kittens stuck inside her in breach position. I held the tiny kitten for hours while Miri was in surgery. Miri knew something was wrong, and she kept bringing me her kitten to care for, and asking for help. If she hadn't had the surgery, she would have died. If I hadn't taken her in, they would have all died.

The operation was a partial success. Miri would be fine but the two kittens didn't survive. The vet offered to find a home for the surviving kitten but I knew I had to keep her. She was as much my baby by then as Miri's. I named her Bijou and she was the sweetest most spoiled cat in the world. She grew up under her mother's watchful eye with Tziki as her playmate. I was a little worried at first. Male cats can be aggressive towards, and even kill kittens, but he was an angel with her. Partly, I believe, because he was terrified of tiny little Miri who would watch them play together with an eagle eye. I never knew for sure if Tziki was Bijou's father, but it's definitely a distinct possibility.

Bijou ruled supreme, whatever she wanted she got. I brought home Magic's winter blanket to wash in the fall. Two dead mice fell out when I pulled in out of the washer and Bijou claimed them, playing with them for hours and hours. When the other two tried to go near them she would growl and hiss at them. It was quite comical to see that tiny kitten barely six weeks old warning off two adult cats significantly larger than her. Even more comical was that they backed off.

As time went by they became more competitive with each other over my attention. I now had three cats and only two hands. But, a few years later, when Bijou got cornered by a street cat the other two went flying to help her. Bijou was an amazing hunter, but she was no fighter. Tziki on the other hand got into fights all the time, and when she needed help, he and her mother had her back.

After I had Tziki neutered he was very aloof and standoffish with me. About six months later he suddenly came up to me asking for attention. I was surprised, and pleased, until I noticed pus on his cheek. I got some supplies and cleaned the area. There was a cat bite on his cheek. I got antibiotics for him through my horse vet, and cleaned the wound every day. He never fussed even though it clearly hurt when I cleaned his wound and no one likes taking medicine. But he had come to me for help and he knew I was helping him, so he let me do what needed to be done. After that his favorite place was on my chest with his face pressed up into my face, purring. I had earned his trust and his love.

The cats followed me as much as they could. I would go for walks with them. There was a grassy area I would start running on, and they would streak past me in excitement tails in the air. They would follow my voice, so when I wanted to leave without them I would rush out silently, they would follow for about 50 ft. then, in the absence of my voice, would turn back.

When Tziki was five he suddenly disappeared for a few days. When he returned he drank a lot but wouldn't eat. Something was clearly wrong. I took him to the vet and found out that he had a urinary tract blockage. He would need special food from then on. It made feeding the cats difficult because Miri wanted his food and I couldn't afford to give it to her. The food he had to eat was three times more expensive than the regular cat food. I had to watch like a hawk while he ate. A year later he disappeared again, this time for over a week. I was sure I would never see him again when he showed up dragging one of his hind legs. I rushed him to the vet, but the vet didn't know what was wrong with him. He gave him something and told me to call in the morning if he wasn't any better. When I called in the morning he told me that my only chance was to take him to the hospital. There was nothing more he could do for him.

Tziki sat there in a frightened daze as they wheeled him around the hospital for testing, and I wanted to rush in to reassure him every time they wheeled him by the glass doors but I wasn't allowed in. the vet finally came out and said they wanted to keep him overnight because he was having trouble breathing. I was hesitant because I knew how afraid of strangers he was. Eventually the vet convinced me to leave him there. I was willing to do whatever it would take to save him. I was making decent money at that time managing a poultry farm, and had few expenses, I was willing to spend every penny I had. They let me go into the ICU for a few minutes. Tziki was huddled up in his cage, terror across his face. I opened the door and started stroking him. Within seconds he was stretched out in complete relaxation purring loudly.

One of the staff walked up and yelled out, "You have to come see this."

None of them could believe the transformation he underwent with me there. As soon as I stopped he went back to huddling in fear in his cage. It was 2 am, and I needed some sleep. I would come back in the morning and spend the rest of the day with him.

As I was getting ready to head back to the hospital the phone rang. Tziki had died overnight. The vet was crying and kept apologizing to me, because Tziki was so scared the whole time, they couldn't treat him. Then she asked to do an autopsy. At first I said no, he was already dead, what good was an autopsy. An hour later I called back and told them to do the autopsy in the hopes that what they found might someday save another cat. The autopsy was conclusive. Tziki had an untreatable heart disease, a hardening of the cardiac muscle. It's possible there are treatments for it today, but, back then there was nothing. People died from it, there was nothing anyone could have done to save him. The news made me feel even worse. I had left him to die alone, afraid, and feeling abandoned for nothing. I know that if I had taken him home he would have died anyways, and I would have felt guilty about not leaving him in the hospital. But that feeling of abandoning him on his deathbed stayed with me until I was setting up my safe space for the EMDR sessions, right before I got my autism diagnosis. My cats were in my safe space, and Tziki ran straight up to me burying his face in mine purring. I knew he had forgiven me, he understood I was trying to help him, but I am still crying over how he died as I type out his story.

My logical brain knows that what I saw as I set up that safe space was what my mind wanted me to see. My cats weren't actually there. But, seeing Tziki in my mind like that helped me break through the 22 year catch 22 I had been in over his death, accept that I had done the right thing, and that I needed to forgive myself over how he died. I had done everything I could for him.

This difficulty forgiving myself is not driven by autism, it is trauma driven. I was conditioned by my parents to believe I was bad, and that every bad thing that happens is totally my fault. Autistic obsessiveness may make me even harder on myself. I fight that notion as much as I can, but when you're autistic and things are constantly going wrong for you, it's a very hard battle.

Two years later Bijou died of the same condition. I knew it was genetic so I had her and Miri tested. Miri was clean, but Bijou had early signs of the disease. A year after I got them tested I took Bijou back to the hospital to see if anything could be done. They gave me some medication and told me that if I kept her indoors, and gave her the medication, she would live longer.

The medication made Bijou sick and being stuck indoors made her very angry. She was constantly trying to sneak out, and she went from being a docile cat to a hissing, spitting and scratching wild animal. After a week I decided it wasn't worth prolonging her life if she was going to be this miserable. When you love someone you sometimes have to let them go. So I stopped giving her the medication, and as soon as the side effects wore off, I opened the door and let her out so she could be happy with whatever time she had left. I was beyond heartbroken when she died, but, I never regretted the decision to stop her medication and let her go outside. She was happy for that last year, and that was the best way I could love her.

When Bijou disappeared, I knew she was dead. Right before she disappeared she came in through the window and loved on me for a few minutes before jumping back out, there was a strange glassy look in her eyes. She knew she was dying and came to say goodbye. I still called for her for days until someone told me there was a dead cat in their yard. I went to look and there she was, moving in the direction of home, one paw stretched out like she was trying to get back to me as she heard me calling her, when her heart stopped.

After Bijou died Miri started exhibiting behaviors she had never exhibited before, they were Bijou's behaviors. When I would come home Bijou would always be on a branch of the tree next to the driveway, and as soon as I turned in she would leap down to greet me. Suddenly Miri was doing this. She would also leap up onto the desk the way Bijou used to. While Bijou was alive Miri never did this. It freaked me out at first because they looked so much alike. I can only speculate that she was trying to take her daughters place to fill the void as best she could. Possibly, she had always wanted to do these things, but Bijou ruled, and with her gone, Miri was able to do them. Having Miri was bittersweet. It was good to have one cat left I could dote on, and pour my love into. But they looked so much alike it was painful. I loved Miri, but not like I loved Bijou. I had raised Bijou from the day she was born, Bijou was my baby.

59

Chapter 9
Back to School

Soon after Tziki died I got a letter from the animal hospital. The hospital was part of the Hebrew University of Jerusalem's veterinary program, though it wasn't in Jerusalem. It was part of a smaller campus in Rehovot, that was across the street from the Weitzman Institute. On the envelope was printed "The Faculty (college) for Agriculture and Environmental Quality Sciences." The words Environmental Quality Sciences stopped me in my tracks. I was an avid environmentalist, very concerned about all the environmental issues that were plaguing the planet. I never knew it was a field of study. It definitely didn't exist when I got out of the military. I started to get excited. This was something I would go back to school for. I rushed over, talked to admissions, got pamphlets and curriculums. It was already summer and the last date I could submit my psychometrics (SAT equivalent), and get in for the upcoming school year was five weeks away, it was less than two months to the beginning of the fall Semester.

There was one exam date left that would get me the results in time, and I got the last available seat for that exam. Now my problem was that it was three weeks away, and I had been out of school for eighteen years. I spent the next three weeks living and breathing psychometric questions. My weakest subject would be the Hebrew, but, because I was going for a science major I knew math would be most important. I spent two weeks relearning most of what I had forgotten from high school. Then I spent the last week working on the Hebrew section. My Hebrew was good enough for day to day life, but they tested us on words no one uses in day to day life. English was no concern. I knew I could pass the English without any studying. Despite my abysmal Hebrew score, I scored in the top 15% for the country. That, with my English, math, and biology, Bagrut grades were enough to get me in.

There was no Environmental Quality Sciences major only a minor. So, I registered for a major in Soil and Water Sciences with a minor in Environmental Quality Sciences. I had no idea when I decided on Soil and Water Sciences that it was the easiest to get into, because very few people applied, but it was the most rigorous curriculum on campus. I liked the course titles in the curriculum. They sounded interesting and seemed to pair well with the environmental quality minor. In Israel you declare your major when you register for university and all the classes you take are related to the degree subject. It is possible to switch majors, but, not without consequences, so switching majors was very rare. Everyone had already had two to five years in the military to figure out the major they wanted.

Before embarking on the task of furthering my education, I had a few things to take care of. I knew I would not be able to continue any of my horse related activities. I found a kibbutz to lend Magic to, and resigned as a show jumping judge.

There was a training competition at a new riding school about a week before my first semester started. I decided to make that my last competition. Because it was a training competition I was working alone and the freedom to be a little more lax with some things, like dress codes. Properly fitting hard hats were required, but I let them substitute white t-shirts for white button down shirts, and rubber boots for leather boots. I wouldn't compromise on safety, but, if a child got disqualified by jumping a wrong jump I could let them finish the round before calling them over and explaining to them what they had done wrong. However, if it was clear the child had lost control over the horse I would immediately ring the bell.

Everything was going well. The course builder, and trainers were all pleased with how I was running things. Then we got to the national level, and I felt it was important to enforce all the rules because these were people who were already competing at the national level, or were about to compete at the national level. They had experience. It wasn't their first or second competition. One girl showed up so sloppily dressed that I called her over and gave her a lecture on respecting the sport, demanded she adjust her chin strap that was way too loose and tuck in her shirt. She tucked in her shirt but refused to adjust the chin strap claiming she didn't know how. I offered to do it for her but her trainer came up and started yelling at me that I was being ridiculous and told the girl to start jumping. I couldn't stop her but I could refuse to judge her and I did. It was a liability issue. If she fell and hurt herself while I was judging her I would be liable. Her chin strap was so loose

61

her helmet would most likely fall off before she hit the ground, it was a serious safety issue. Her horse started refusing one of the jumps over and over again.

The competition organizer came to talk to me. I explained I wasn't judging her and why, and he agreed. Her trainer started attacking me, saying the jump was too high, and that instead of demanding things like tucked in shirts and chin straps I should have measured that jump and deemed it unsuitable. This was incorrect. Riders and trainers get to walk the course before the competition begins and they have the right to dispute a jump based on height. As a judge it was my job to look for dangers like a jump that would hurt the horse and/or rider if they knocked it down.

Then something happened I had never seen before. The course builder and all the other trainers started yelling at the trainer who was yelling at me. They all took my side and demanded he and his student leave the arena. It was a great way to end my career as a show jumping judge, but it also made me sad to be leaving.

I moved to Rehovot where the campus was located soon after being accepted to the university. I found an apartment to rent with two other girls who were starting school at the faculty that year, and got a job working campus security. The apartment didn't work out. The other two girls were friends, and they didn't like me, so I ended up getting kicked out. I eventually found a tiny 1 bedroom in a nearby town, in an elderly woman's backyard where I stayed until I moved back to the US.

The best thing about the security position was that I had to do hourly rounds through the buildings for some shifts. I loved walking through the academic buildings. The walls were covered with posters from past research projects and I would read them as I went through the buildings. I spent the most time in the Soil and Water Sciences building soaking up as much information as I could. One day as I stood reading a poster one of the professors, YC, walked out of his lab and started talking to me. He was all smiles over my enthusiasm, and wished me luck.

One night I was alone in a security spot watching the bats fly around. I heard a strange high pitched noise coming from a distance. I couldn't figure out where it was coming from, so when another security officer came by on his rounds to check up on me, I asked if he knew where the sound was coming from. He gave a strange look and said he heard nothing. I could tell he thought I was making it up or hearing things so I didn't ask about it anymore. I never found out what it was, but I know I heard it. It is quite common for autistics to hear things others don't hear. This is part of our sensory profile. We have to deal with more noise input because our hearing tends to be more acute.

Two weeks after the school year started a research assistant position opened up in the Soil and Water Sciences. YC ran into me in the hallway again and suggested I apply for the position. I immediately applied but didn't get the job. They wanted a second year student who would have a better background in the subject. I was disappointed but understood their position. A week after being turned down for the position I ran into YC in the hallway again. He told me he had heard that I didn't get the position and asked me to come to his office the next day. I was nervous but showed up, and after asking me a few questions he offered me a research assistant position in his lab. Within a month of starting school, I was a research assistant. My job was with someone who worked at another facility who was collaborating with YC on a research project. I would still be working in YC's lab but under the direct supervision of the other researcher who was rarely there. I also had to help with cleaning glassware and other tasks YC's lab manager would give me to help her.

The main portion of my job was to extract the organic matter from the soil matrix for analysis. They were going to compare organic matter parameters from different types of soil. What they were looking for I do not remember. I just remember having to extract organic matter from several different types of soil, and running some of the tests towards the end.

One of the grad students pointed out to me that one of the soil types was extremely poor quality, and that the amount of organic matter in it was extremely low. On top of that it was very high in calcium carbonate so that by the time I would remove all the calcium carbonate there wouldn't be much left. I was unlikely to get enough to run any tests on. I asked him if we could use more soil on these samples, and he said, "No, it has to be a uniform 20 grams of soil for each extraction or the chemistry won't work."

The entire extraction method was based on 20 grams of soil. Then I asked if there was a way to measure how much calcium carbonate was in each sample so we could calculate how much to add in order to have 20 grams of the soil left after removing the calcium carbonate. That way the chemistry would work, and we could provide the calculations so any testing could be adjusted to take that into account if needed.

The grad student thought my suggestion was brilliant, so we tested, and logged the amount of calcium carbonate for each soil depth, and how much soil I should use for use depth to end up with 20 grams of actual soil. The only thing I would have to change in the entire process was the initial amount of soil and the amount of hydrochloric acid needed to remove all the calcium carbonate. He wanted to name the methodology after me. I suggested we name it for both of us since it was a joint effort. I had come up with the original idea, and he put together the method. I didn't know enough chemistry at the time to create a method or make any of the calculations. After all I was six weeks into my first semester in university. The methodology never got named, but it was still a moment of glory.

I became a soil organic matter extracting machine. The previous student would work on one sample to completion before starting to work on another. But, there were some very long boring periods where the samples had to go through a process that lasted anywhere from days to weeks, and there would be nothing for me to do other than periodically check and make sure everything was still running. I decided to do it assembly line style, starting a new batch as soon as the last one hit a slow stage, moving from batch to batch performing different stages of the extraction process on different soil samples, using a spreadsheet to keep my supervisor appraised of everything I was doing.

My lack of knowledge caused me to make a few mistakes along the way but none of them were catastrophic. I didn't know to use the plastic droppers for the hydrofluoric acid. It took a few months for me to understand my mistake, and it explained the strange cloudiness of the glass droppers after I used them. Those of you who know what hydrofluoric acid does are chuckling right now. You might be thinking of the scene in Breaking Bad where Jesse puts the body in the bathtub instead of a plastic tub. I watched that scene in horror knowing what was about to happen. The way it played out in the movie was of course completely unscientific. Jesse and Walt would have both died if that had happened.

Most of the work was with chemicals that were fairly innocuous. I loved watching the mist of carbon dioxide and water that come out of the soil samples when I added the hydrochloric acid to them. But hydrofluoric acid is extremely dangerous. The lab manager told me that the previous student wouldn't wear gloves, and he almost died when a drop landed on his finger. They rushed him to the hospital in time but it was a very close call. One drop of hydrofluoric acid can kill a person. After that I was even more conscientious of wearing my safety gear when handling the hydrofluoric acid, and making sure there was someone in the lab whenever I handled it, just in case. I even had a classmate come to the lab with me once late at night so I could do the procedure safely. She wouldn't know what to do if there was an accident, but she could call 114 (911).

The work started to become repetitive and tedious after a few months but I stuck with it. I was getting so much more than just lab experience from that job. One of the grad students invited to join the weekly graduate seminars, and I gladly went. I was like an information sponge, soaking up every little bit of information I could, from anywhere I could. On top of that, the first topic was related to climate change and that was a topic I was very interested in.

YC looked surprised when I walked into that first graduate seminar but never said anything. I sat through it in a daze not understanding anything I was hearing. Everyone else was asking questions and having heated debates and I had no idea what any of it was about beyond the fact that it had something to do with climate change. I confided in the grad student who had invited me and she said, "Just keep going, you'll figure it out over time."

So I kept going. The topics kept changing, but, I slowly started to grasp what the speakers were saying. About a month after my first seminar, I understood enough to have a question. I raised my hand, YC looked surprised again, but said nothing.

Asking the question was harder than I thought. I was having a hard time getting my thoughts into verbal words. This is completely different from my situational mutism. Because autistics process information at a different rate than allistics we sometimes get stuck trying to verbalize a new idea that is in our heads. Our brains are so busy dealing with massive amounts of sensory input that it gets in the way. But I managed to formulate a comprehensible question, and to my surprise, the lecturer said, "That's an excellent question."

I was worried I would get laughed at for asking such a simple question. I glanced over at YC, and he was beaming. I realize now that he had taken a huge risk asking a first semester student to work in his lab, and it was paying off for him. I continued to go to the graduate seminars, and any other seminars I was able to attend. Over time I learned to ask better, and better questions. I was learning to think like a scientist.

By the middle of my first semester everyone had gotten so used to seeing me around that they assumed I was a grad student. This was partly because I was going to the graduate seminars, and partly because of the long hours I was working in the lab. Normally students were allowed to work up to 20 hours a week. I couldn't make ends meet on 20 hours a week. I told YC I was going to look for another job and that it might affect my times in the lab. He asked me if more hours would help, and I said yes but didn't see how it was possible. But YC had a lot of clout on campus, and he got permission for me to work up to 30 hours a week while school was in session. I was able to scrape by on that. I couldn't afford a lot of things, like heat in the winter, or cooking gas (I became very adept at cooking with an electric kettle). But I managed. I would do my homework in the winter wearing layers and my winter coat, using a cup of hot water to warm my hands. My bed was piled with blankets and quilts, and I had the two cats to help keep me warm. I looked for scholarships, but they all had a cutoff age of 30. I couldn't get financial aid because I had a car. Giving up the car would mean I couldn't work, so that was a catch 22. I often stayed in the lab until midnight to get my hours in. I was starting to really struggle, something had to be removed from my schedule.

The program I was in required 165 credits to graduate, and it was a three year program. First year students had their schedule set for the first year, then each got to choose their schedule based on the program requirements and their interests. I was taking 32 semester credits and working 30 hours a week plus several hours of homework a day, and homework all day Saturday. I decided to divide my degree into four years so I could take off a few credits per semester. It was still a big load but it was more manageable.

To my surprise grad students started coming to the lab to ask me questions about their research. I kept saying, "I don't know."

After this happened a few times I finally asked one of them if he knew I was a first year student. He was stunned, and that was when I realized everyone thought I was a grad student. I was in fact leaps and bounds ahead of my classmates because of everything I was learning at work, but I was still a first year undergrad. During the first semester my classmates all teased me about working during my first semester. It was a very uncommon thing to do. But, by the second semester, when they had realized how much I was getting from my work, they were all scrambling to find jobs in a research lab.

My advantage started to dawn on them when I was able to secure the seminar room for our additional math tutoring. I was struggling with calculus. The professor had a thick Russian accent, and his instruction was somewhat baffling. To make matters worse he would constantly say, "And you remember this from high school." Everyone would be nodding yes, and I would be shaking my head no. I remembered nothing from high school and the math for the psychometric had not included any calculus. Because we were so far from main campus, and there was no math program on our campus, we had no TA (teaching assistant). The professor taught the practice sessions. Usually the TA is a grad student and can bring things "down to earth" and make them understandable. All we were getting was more of the incomprehensible explanations we received in class. We were all struggling. Like many professors our math professor knew a lot about his subject matter, but he didn't know how to teach it. Several of my classmates complained and the university found us a TA from the Weitzman Institute. All we needed was a room, and I was able to secure that.

The first time we walked into the seminar room everyone was oohing and ahhing at the soil profiles displayed in the room. We had a few classmates that didn't want the soil and water program. They had joined in the hopes of being able to transfer to biotechnology which was much harder to get into because of the high demand. First year classes for soil and water were the closest to the first year classes for biotechnology, so it was the only major they had a chance of transferring from. One of them took one look at the soil profiles and said, "I am definitely in the wrong major."

Our excitement over "a bunch of dirt" baffled her. We laughed and told her she would soon be rid of us, but she was still with us in the second year, and the "dirt" was starting to grow on her.

Math suddenly started to make sense again. The TA was able to explain things in a way that made sense and we were all doing better.

Without the TA from the Weitzman Institute, we probably would have all failed calculus.

Chemistry was my favorite subject, except for the labs. I loved working in a lab, but lab classes were a drag. The experiments were boring, and we had to write lengthy reports on each one. That wouldn't have been too bad except for one thing. We worked in pairs, and every two pairs had to submit a report. The amount of work involved in a report was based on four people working on it. My lab partner was great, and she worked hard, but the other pair did nothing. We had to carry them the entire semester. We complained to the TA's but they said it was our problem. So my lab partner and I did all the work, and they got our grades, until we got to the last lab. After each lab we would collect their data to incorporate into our report, but this time, they had no data. They had a problem with their experiment and had no data to share. We appealed to the TA's again but to no avail. They told us that if we didn't submit a report with two sets of data we would get a failing grade on the report.

Later that day, as I was grinding soil in the lab fume hood with a mortar and pestle, visualizing the chemistry TA's faces each time I pushed the pestle down, I heard a rustling of papers, YC was in his office. Between his travels, and teaching commitments he was rarely in his office. I continued to grind for a while, trying to muster the courage to ask him for advice.

After about an hour I finally got the courage to knock on YC's door. I explained the problem and asked him for advice. YC agreed that the TA's were being unreasonable.

"Have you talked to the professor in charge of the class?" YC asked.

I admitted that it had not occurred to me. He told me go talk to him, and that everything would get sorted out.

I went over to the chemistry building, but, the professor was out, so I talked to his administrative assistant. She said she would convey the message, but I could tell she wasn't taking me seriously. I decided to tell her that I had talked to YC and that he had advised me to talk to the chemistry professor. I thought that having the back up of another professor would get her, and him, to take me more seriously. Her eyes popped open and her face turned white when I mentioned YC's name. She became very nervous and told me to come back in two hours, and I started to feel hopeful. Mentioning another professor was the right thing to do.

When I came back two hours later the professor was in, and he was practically bending over backwards to be helpful. He promised me that everything would be fine, that I didn't have to submit a report, he was going to do something else instead to get us our final grade. Until that moment I didn't realize just how much clout YC had on campus. I later found out that YC had been the campus dean for many years, that he was the most respected professor on campus, and a giant in his field.

During the summer I worked full time in the lab and had a series of other jobs to help me make ends meet during the next school year. The first odd job was at a cactus pear farm. The work itself wasn't difficult but the working conditions were brutal. We had to wear massive amounts of protective gear so we wouldn't be covered in needles all the time, and we had to work at night because it was impossible to wear all that gear in the daytime during the summer. We picked three nights a week, 12 hour shifts. The job paid double what I made per hour in my lab job, and it was in cash after each shift. I worked four tens in the lab so I could do both jobs and for a while it was working out well, though, despite all the gear we wore the tiny needles still got through and I was covered in them. Each time I would pick something up the pain from the needles in my fingertips would make my eyes mist.

I had started working at the cactus pear farm alongside another classmate, but she dropped out after a few shifts. The gear, long hours, and needles were too much for her. I continued working on my own with the owner. After about a month my boss at the cactus pear farm came on to me. I was scared, and completely uninterested. So I took my money that day and never went back. I had no idea how to navigate that situation. I had a boss come on to me about a decade earlier when I was working in the airline industry, and ended up getting fired right after turning him down. My go to in situations I couldn't handle was to run.

I had made a fair amount of money working at the cactus pear farm but there was still about six weeks left to the summer break and I needed to make more to get me through the next year. I found a weekend job cleaning out animal cages at a zoo. They had regular staff who would clean the cages during the week but needed people to fill in on the weekend. Weekends in Israel were one day, Saturday. The work week, and school, ran from Sunday to Friday.

At first I was assigned to the lemurs, and raccoons. There were a few other animals but those are the ones I remember because they were so cute. I fell in love with the lemurs, and wanted a lemur for a pet. I started sneaking in treats to give to them. They quickly started taking the food out of my hands. Hands down the lemurs were my favorites. I had to be more careful with the raccoons. I still gave them treats, but not directly from my hands.

***

This was not my first time working at a zoo. At one point I was teaching kids in a kibbutz horseback riding on the ponies they had in the kibbutz petting zoo. I tried to make the lessons about more than just riding, so I had the kids dress up the ponies for Purim and parade them for the community. Then we participated in the parade for Shavuot, the harvest festival. I also trained one of the fillies to pull a carriage even though I had never done that before. But, I had a natural sense for working with horses and was able to figure out the steps.

My big fascination at that petting zoo was the baboons. I found their interactions fascinating. One day a crate of fish arrived while I was finishing up with the ponies. The fish were for the water fowl. The petting zoo was in a migratory corridor, and people would bring them injured birds to be nursed back to health. Some birds had injuries that made it impossible for them to return to the wild so they stayed at the petting zoo permanently. I took the smallest fish from the crate and dropped it into the baboons' food chute, curious to see how they would handle it. The little ones came up first sniffing the fish but not knowing what they do with it. Then the male came, scattering the others, and picked up the fish. The male was a tyrant, constantly abusing the female baboons, and even the youngsters. So I was shocked, and in awe of what happened next.

The male baboon sat down with the fish and started turning it over in his hands sniffing at it, trying to figure out how to tackle it. After a few minutes, he started pulling off the scales with his teeth. The little ones, ranging from two years to a few weeks old sat in a perfect semi circle around him, as if they were in a classroom. One by one they would walk up to take a closer look and then go back to their spot in the semi circle. At no time did two of them go at the same time. They seemed to have a preset order, though I saw no logic in the order they were going, or any sign of communication. It simply worked. The male never got aggressive, as if he knew they were just trying to learn from him, maybe he was even enjoying the role of teacher. Normally walking up to him while he was eating would result in a life threatening beating. The scenario continued until the male finished consuming the fish. I could see how closely related our species were watching that scenario play out.

***

I would have been happy staying with the lemurs and raccoons the rest of the summer but after a few weeks they moved me to the iguanas. I hated the iguanas. They would whiplash with their tails, and it was painful. Then I had the flamingos and parrots which wasn't too bad. But I wanted to go back to the lemurs.

The zoo didn't pay as much as the cactus pear farm so I started tutoring a twelve year old girl who was failing math. The first thing I did was take away her calculator, so she could get a feel for numbers. I insisted she do the calculations by hand, and she had to show me the process. They were working on fractions and decimals but to my surprise they hadn't learned long division. There was no way I could think of to explain how you got from 1/3 to 0.333 or, 1/8 to 0.125 without long division, so I taught her how to do long division. Then I had her dividing 1 by two, one by 3, etc. to show her how a fraction and decimal have the same value. She was very intelligent and caught on quickly. I was clearly doing something right because she aced her next math exam. Like me, she just needed a different approach to math than what she was getting in school. Unfortunately very soon after that exam her parents accused me of saying something I never said. We probably could have worked it out but I got upset, went nonverbal, left, and never went back. I never tutored again.

When you are constantly being misunderstood, and being accused of saying things you never said, even small things become intolerable. I was becoming more and more sensitive to these types of misunderstanding with every passing year. There are two ways to break a rock. One is with a sledgehammer, the other is with the slow but continuous drip, drip, drip of water that slowly erodes it. This is what often happens to autistics. That drip, drip, drip of misunderstandings was eroding my confidence, my tolerance, and my overall mental health. Not knowing I was autistic, and not understanding that autistic overwhelm was what was driving me during these misunderstandings made coping much harder.

In my second year YC taught a graduate class on soil organic matter. In Israel all you needed to take a graduate class as an undergrad was permission from the professor. I asked YC if I could take his class and he agreed enthusiastically. So in my third semester I was taking a graduate level soils class, along with my introduction to soil sciences class. I was the only undergrad in the class.

I loved YC's approach to teaching. He cared more about us understanding concepts than memorizing data. For our homework assignments we would get a problem, and we would have to set our own parameters to solve it. As long as we set the parameters correctly, and did the correct math with those parameters, the answer was correct. We could make our parameters as simple or complicated as we wanted. The only caveat was that they had to work in agreement. If you set parameters that conflicted with each other in any way, you failed. I always went for the easiest set of parameters. Most of the others did too. One grad student, the one who had invited me to that first graduate seminar would use more complex parameters. She wanted more of a challenge. She was a genius.

One day YC gave us a trick question for homework. I started solving it in a straightforward way but the answer I got didn't make sense to me. I double checked and triple checked my math but kept getting the same answer. Something wasn't right. I decided to walk away from it and go back to it later with the hopes of getting some insight. The solution came to me quickly. It was a qualitative question not a quantitative question. There was no math, just a concept. For those of you who want to know I will explain the question and answer. If this doesn't interest you, skip the next paragraph, it's a little technical.

We were given a leaching rate of soil organic matter from the solid soil matrix to the surrounding soil liquid. The entire soil was contained in a plastic barrier. We were asked to provide the amount of soil organic matter that moved out of the soil in 24 hours. I originally thought the plastic barrier was there to simplify the math. However, the number I was getting with the math was so infinitesimally small, that I questioned it. It was so small that asking the question didn't make sense, it was statistically null. The concept YC was looking for was that there was no change because both the solid and the liquid were part of the soil. The entire class had realized there was a problem with the mathematical solution. I know this because there was a lot of discussion about that one question right before class. Only a few of us figured out on our own what the answer was. The rest were asking for guidance.

As I walked to class the day that homework was due, one of my fellow classmates called out to me in the hallway asking if I had done my homework. When I said yes, she asked me about the above question I had struggled with. I explained the answer to her. Through the corner of my eye, I saw one of the girls who had gotten me kicked out of that first apartment in Rehovot. She and her friend had written me off as a loser. She stood there, eyes popping, and jaw dropped. The grad student I was talking to was her TA in another class, and there I was, explaining a homework problem for a class we were clearly taking together. I continued walking with the grad student to class, savoring the look on that girl's face. I felt vindicated.

I did well in the graduate class scoring the second highest grade in the class. But things were eroding fast. My financial situation was getting to me. I was angry over the fact that I couldn't get any financial aid just because I had a small fifteen year old car. When Bijou died towards the end of my first year some options opened up for me. Until that point I refused to consider them because I knew she couldn't survive the trip. I filled out a FAFSA form and found out that, based on my income, I could go to school in the US without having to pay tuition. It would all be paid for with federal grants. I started applying to schools, was already accepted at a few, and decided to move back to the US after my third semester so I could get settled in wherever I would end up going. I could work in the interim to make things easier once the school year started.

My decision to skip a semester was based on logistics. The school year in Israel ran from around October to end of June, then we had exams for a month. I wouldn't have time to get acclimated and settled in before the school year started in the US around mid-August, or any time to work and save up some money. YC was very unhappy about my decision. I think he had plans for me to do my graduate work with him. But I was worn out, and feeling discriminated against because of my age. I had served my country but I couldn't even get the money other students got when they went to university because it was over five years since I finished my service. Every avenue I explored to get help led to a dead end, and I was tired of living with no heat in the winter or cooling in the summer, or being able to take a day off, and the myriad of other things I was denying myself.

A few weeks before I was supposed to leave I got into an argument with the lab manager. She told me in no uncertain terms that if I didn't do what she had asked I was fired, and I said fine. I was leaving soon anyways. About two months earlier I had taken the initiative to deep clean the lab. It was a Friday, and I always worked all day Friday because I had no classes. Most of the grad students were gone for the weekend. It was the perfect day to tackle the project. I spent all day moving equipment, emptying and reorganizing shelves and cabinets. Every so often YC would walk out of his office to give me an encouraging smile. The lab was spotless by the time I was done. It was so clean that one grad student walked in and walked right out Sunday morning thinking she had walked into the wrong lab. Within a day the lab was a mess. The graduate students seemed to almost go out of their way to create clutter and dirt. I swore to myself that I would never do it again. So when the lab manager asked me to do it again, I refused. I probably escalated things by not being able to explain why I was refusing but, though I didn't know it at the time, I was in overwhelm, and having trouble talking. All I could say was no. It can't have been easy for people around me to see me suddenly change when I was nearing a meltdown, or in a meltdown. It wasn't easy for me either, but I had no understanding of what was happening to me, and no way to explain. Not even to myself. Until recently I didn't even realize just how bad my behavior can get at those times. It's embarrassing to think about it.

The on campus environmental activist group I was in was mad at me for leaving. We were in the middle of a campaign, and they needed me. So I ended up leaving campus with everyone mad at me.

While I left campus on bad terms, I left the tiny house I was living in on excellent terms. I gave the woman I was renting from some items I couldn't take with me, and she insisted I not pay rent the last month, and that I take one of her paintings as a parting gift. She had started painting at age 70, and was remarkably skilled. She asked me to pick from a variety of paintings she had in her studio, and I picked a very small painting of a rose. I didn't have much room in my suitcases, and it was enough to remind me of her kindness towards me.

74

Chapter 10
Back to the US

I had to pack everything into two suitcases. A lot of hard choices had to be made about what I was keeping and what I wasn't. Most people ship the rest of their things but I didn't have the money to do that, so whatever I couldn't take with me, except the car which I sold, I gave away or donated to charity. Thankfully I would be able to take Miri on the plane with me, I just had to pay for her and the price was per pound. When they weighed her at the airport she weighed two lbs. so it was a cheap ticket. Did I mention she was a tiny cat.

Before I left I had to get Magic settled. I couldn't sell him. That would mean losing all control over him, and I had promised him when I bought him that I would never sell him. The story of black beauty was weighing on my mind. Even though it has a happy ending the horse went through a lot of abuse before he got there, and I didn't want Magic to go through anything like that. I was not happy with what I saw when I went to visit him at the kibbutz I had loaned him to. They couldn't handle him, and he had become almost as wild as he was when I first bought him, so I knew I couldn't keep him there. The friend I had left him with who told me he was a jumper was starting her own riding school. I called her, and she was thrilled to have him. Right before I left I went to see him one last time. He was calm and content. My friend told me she was using him as her schoolmaster, and that he was wonderful. He was about twelve at the time, and I knew he would have a happy home for life there. I could leave him there with a clear conscience. Even if the school failed she would keep him for her own children to ride. I wasn't sure when, or if, I was going to make it back. Tickets weren't cheap and they haven't gotten any cheaper.

With the meager funds I had, I decided to move in with my parents when I arrived hoping things would be better now that I was older and getting a degree. I even thought for a very short while that I would be able to stay with them while I finished my degree and save some money. My parents had two spare rooms so technically it wouldn't be a problem.

It was several years since I had been to visit the US. The last time I went for Passover at my parents' request, they sent me a plane ticket, it was such a disaster that I didn't want to go again. It wasn't my first traumatizing Passover and I didn't want any repeat performances.

***

By the time I landed In New York I had been awake for over 24 hours. All I wanted was to go back to the house and get some sleep. But my parents wanted us all to go to dinner together at a restaurant that was over an hour's drive away. My request to be dropped off at the house was denied. My father was hungry and when my father was hungry that was that. It was almost midnight New York time when I finally got to go to sleep. Since I was sleeping on the living room couch, I had to wait for everyone else to go to sleep. I always slept on the couch even though it was bad for my back. At two am I woke up and couldn't go back to sleep. It was 8 am in Israel, and I never slept past 8 am. Everyone was sleeping so I found a 300 piece puzzle to work on until they woke up, and finished it soon after they all got up.

The rest of the day, I did everything I was asked to do. By the time we lit the holiday candles I could barely keep my eyes open. It was after midnight in Israel. I went into my parents' bedroom to get some sleep. The smells were strange, and my mother was talking loudly to someone in the next room, so by the time I fell asleep, my father and brothers were returning from services and my mother came to wake me up. I said I was too tired and needed sleep. After that, one by one, they each came in to shake me awake and tell me to come to the table. I finally got up grabbed the keys to my father's car and went to sleep in the car. When I woke up the Seder was over, my back was hurting, and I went upstairs to the couch to try and sleep a few more hours.

The next day I couldn't stand up. My back had gone from bad to worse and all I could do was crawl on all four to get what I needed like go to the bathroom. I set up some blankets on the floor to work on my back, try to ease it but it would take time. Around noon my father started screaming at me because I wasn't helping. There was no reasoning with him so I crawled around on all four doing what I could, and crying. I was thirty years old, still being treated like a child.

Years later I confronted my father about that incident. He said that he thought I was just acting up. In fact, both my parents admitted that they always thought I was just acting up whenever I would say something was hurting me.

***

Unfortunately, nothing had actually changed. My mother was 'thrilled' to have me there, but when it came to accommodating my needs, I was out of luck. They put me in the smaller room that was right off the kitchen. That on its own would have been fine, except that there was a TV right outside the door that my mother would blast whenever she was in the kitchen, and I couldn't handle the noise. There was no way I could work with the TV pounding my head. I asked to move to the other room but was told it was my father's office and I could only have the room I was in. My father had two offices, and he rarely used that one. When my brother was studying for the bar he spent six months in that room, but I wasn't good enough. The office electronics my father had in there could be moved to the other room so my father could access them anytime, and I could have some peace and quiet, but that was asking for too much. I had to find a place of my own.

The only school I hadn't heard back from yet was Rutgers, and of the schools I had applied to, that was my first choice. I looked at Princeton and Cornell but was afraid to commit to the price tag. I didn't think the grants I would be getting would cover that much. So I applied to several state universities, and they all accepted me as a transfer student, except the one I wanted the most. I wanted Rutgers because the courses they offered looked interesting. Later I would find out that most of the courses in the catalogue weren't offered any more. Anxious for an answer I went to the main campus to find the admissions office and find out what was happening with my application. They said they were missing some paperwork I had already submitted, so I resubmitted, and I was in.

Armed with my acceptance letter I started looking for a research assistant position. After a few weeks I found one in the entomology department, applied, and was hired. It wasn't the department I wanted but it would do until I found something better. The projects I was involved with had to do with grass grubs and hemlock aphids that were both invasive species that were doing a lot of damage to their hosts and needed better controls. The best part of the job was that it was mostly out in the field. The insects we had to handle weren't too scary and I quickly got used to them.

My supervisor, J, was Chinese. I had never known anyone who was Chinese before, so it was exciting to learn a little bit about Chinese culture from him. We exchanged stories, taught each other a few phrases in our respective languages, and J would take me with him during breaks to Chinese food stores where he introduced me to a lot of foods I had never heard of before. I still use the tofu skins he introduced me to all those years ago. I didn't eat most of the foods, he just explained what they were. I liked J and felt very comfortable around him which was a relief because I felt completely alienated from the other students. Maybe it was the fact that I was much closer in age to J than the other students. Maybe the fact that we came from different cultures, and were open to learning about each other's cultures that made me comfortable. Maybe it was both. J was also very happily married, and never made me uncomfortable in that regard. I was rarely comfortable with men anymore.

***

While I still had Strider I started doing weekly trail rides with a young man, N, who had a stallion he kept in another DIY barn. He had never learned to ride, just did what felt instinctively right, so I would give him tips whenever we were out together. I had no romantic interest in him, we were just friends. N had a girlfriend so it didn't seem to be an issue. We rode together for several years.

One Friday while I was washing Magic, he pulled up in his car to ask if I wanted to ride the next day. I said, "Sure."

We set a time, and he drove off. His girlfriend had been standing next to the car looking annoyed the whole time, but I thought nothing of it. The next day while we were riding, he told me that his girlfriend had told him that, if she ever saw me again she would slap me. I was shocked, but also found it very amusing. I had no clue as to what I could have done during that short exchange to make her react like that, so I shrugged it off, and I never saw her again.

About a year later a rose was delivered to me at work with a note saying "from a secret admirer." I have to admit, I thought it was exciting, until two days later N showed up holding a rose. It was a very uncomfortable exchange, because I still had no romantic interest in him. I suddenly understood his girlfriend's comment. She must have picked up on a vibe from him that made her jealous of me.

A few years later I was working at a remote private horse farm, N showed up. He was friends with the guy who had previously managed the farm. They wanted to go out riding the next day, so N asked if he could stay at my place. I had a large studio at the farm with a couch he could sleep on, so I offered him the couch. I woke up in the middle of the night with N on top of me. It took a few seconds for my sleepy brain to process what was happening then I shoved him off me and screamed at him to get out.

I was about thirty when that happened. I've always felt embarrassed that it took me a few seconds to get him off me, as if I was condoning his actions when I first woke up. I keep berating myself for not throwing him out quicker. After that experience I found it very difficult to have male friends, and would respond very strongly whenever a man I wasn't interested in showed the slightest interest in me. So for me to feel comfortable around J was huge, and he was always a perfect gentleman with me.

My boss at the horse farm told me N was banned from the farm, but his friend managed to blame me for something he did a few weeks later, and got me fired. My boss took his word over mine. I had to find a new job and a new place to live.

***

I decided to find a weekend job to supplement my earnings, I only had a few months before school started and I wanted to make sure I had enough money put away to be able to afford things like heat. I found a weekend job at a Dunkin Donuts. I hated it, the other workers never accepted me, but I stuck with it until the school year started.

I had to have a car so I found an old Hyundai that could barely go up to 60 mph for $400.00. It was ugly, but it would get me to where I needed to go. I had that car for three years. After it died I found a slightly better car for $600.00.

A month before school started I found a place with another student. I took over the lease from another student who had graduated and was going home. We ended up staying there for a few months until the lease ran out, and decided not to renew because of our neighbors. We found a new place together. It was larger so we brought in a series of third roommates over the years we lived there.

I was walking along a busy street one day, stopped at a crosswalk and was looking around as I waited for the light to turn green. It suddenly hit me that most of the people around me weren't Jewish. Growing up in Israel I just took for granted that almost everyone was Jewish, and never gave it any thought. For the first time in my life, I was the minority. I asked myself if it mattered that the people around me weren't Jewish, and quickly got the response that, no it doesn't matter, people are people, it makes no difference. Then a more difficult question popped into my head "does it matter to me that I am Jewish?" My initial reaction was the same, people are people it doesn't matter. But something inside me told me that I needed to examine this more carefully.

A few days later I realized that it did matter. It mattered a lot. Not because it made me different, but because so many of my ancestors had died to keep this identity alive, and I would be spitting on their graves if I didn't care about it. Years later this would be a discussion topic in an Israeli group I went to, and we all said the same thing. None of us were religious, but, out of deference to our ancestors' sacrifices, our Jewish identities mattered.

College in the US was nothing like University in Israel. Nothing in the US was like Israel. The first time I went to put mail in a mailbox I stood in front of it for ten minutes unsure if I had the right box or how to put the mail in. I started wondering how people who came to the US who weren't fluent In English managed because I was finding everything so difficult, including the people. What I didn't know was that, being autistic, change is often much more difficult for me than most other people. It has to do with sensory input, information processing, and possibly a few other things I don't yet understand. Small changes lead to overwhelm. Too much change can lead to meltdowns, shutdown, and even suicidality. Each autistic has their own threshold of how much change they can handle, and it's a moving threshold. Other stressors affect the amount of change we can handle. I get upset when packaging of a food item changes. The words "new and improved" fill me with dread. I spent my whole life silently railing against all these changes, not understanding why they were so difficult for me to accept.

Professors in Israel had the attitude of 'you are adults and you are responsible for your own time and actions.' No one ever took attendance, our homework was for us to practice, and learn from, it didn't count towards our grade. Only finals counted. This is probably why our finals were spaced out over a month instead of the week in the US. We also had two dates so if you weren't happy with your grade or couldn't make the first date, you could take it on the second date. So, for faculty, exams were always spread over two months. There were even third dates for reserve soldiers who had been in service during the semester. The third dates were arranged privately, and you had to have served a certain number of days, or be in service during exams, to get a special third date. We had one girl in our class in Israel who never went to a single lecture. She studied on her own from the books and aced every exam. So when I started school in the US and suddenly everyone was taking attendance, and you couldn't miss more than three classes or your grade dropped, I was taken aback. It made me not want to be there.

As I mentioned earlier, autistics have a built in defiance to being told what to do. It's not as severe as oppositional defiance disorder, and there are ways to get around it, at least for me, but it's there, and like our difficulties with change, it's driven by processing differences, and sensory issues. I would always do better when left to my own devices as much as possible. Without constant supervision I start to drive myself. The more I am managed the less productive I become because I'm expending too much energy trying to overcome the blocks this creates in my brain. I never understood why I struggled with supervision until after I got my autism diagnosis, I just knew I needed maximum autonomy to perform well. In fact, the only downside to my diagnoses is that I am not so 'special' anymore. Suddenly there are explanations for all the little quirks I thought made me special. I am meeting other people like me, and it's now just autism. In order for me to accept change I have to understand the rationale for it. It's still difficult but much easier to handle when I can rationalize to myself why I need to deal with the change. If I can't rationalize the need to change, and am not given a rational reason when I ask for one, change becomes intolerable. None of the differences between university in Israel and college in the US made any sense to me, so I struggled with them, and resented them. I started getting some C's for the first time since going back to school, and much of the joy I got from being in school dissipated. School started feeling like a chore again.

Having our homework count towards our final grade was another difficult adjustment. Homework was meant to be a learning exercise, not something that counted for a permanent grade. I was suddenly expected to get everything right the first time, there was no room for error. I think the intent was to take pressure off finals, but for me, it just added pressure. In my second semester at Hebrew University our organic chemistry professor wasn't giving us homework assignments. After about three weeks I went to talk to him after a lecture. He told me there were exercises in the book that I could do on my own. I explained that I wanted my homework graded so I could learn from it. It was also hard to get motivated once I had finished all my other homework unless I had a specific assignment. He came up with a compromise, and started giving homework assignments, but made them optional to hand in. I was the only one in my major who handed in the homework assignments. Everyone was laughing at me but I didn't care. The first one came back covered in red ink. But, each subsequent one came back with less red ink. Half the class failed organic chemistry, most of the others barely passed, only a handful of us got good grades. My final grade was 97, the girl who studied alone got the only 100. No one was laughing at me anymore. Everyone was asking me to help them study for the second exam.

I understand that incorporating homework into final grades is meant to encourage people to do the homework, but, there are better ways to do that. For example, our Hebrew U calculus professor wouldn't let anyone take the final unless they had submitted a certain number of homework assignments. That allowed us to use the homework as a learning tool while ensuring it got done.

I had to take an English writing class before I was able to take composition 101. I took it as a pass fail, learned as much as I could, and signed up for composition 101 where I discovered that everything I had learned about writing in the previous class was wrong. Composition 101 was an interesting experience. Everyone had told me to go take it at a community college to make it easier. It was one of those classes that automatically transferred, but was significantly harder to take at Rutgers than a community college. The fact that everyone was telling me it was hard at Rutgers made we want to take it at Rutgers. I seem to do well in hard classes and struggle in easy ones. Probably because the easy ones don't interest me. I need to either be interested in the topic, or feel challenged to do well. I got a D on my first assignment and I was upset. I had used everything I had learned in the previous English writing class. When I realized that everything I had learned there was wrong my grades started to get better. I was later able to go back and edit my original essays and resubmit them. I was amazed at how much editing I had to do on them. The composition I got a D on was so bad that I didn't know how to begin editing it, so I kept that grade, and ended up with a B+ in Composition 101. I was satisfied with that.

There were a lot of unscientific classes I needed to take to get my degree at Rutgers. At Hebrew U we weren't allowed to take anything that didn't directly pertain to our major. There were electives, but they were all science based. I hated the idea of having to take humanities classes and did my best to stay away from them. I ended up taking a ceramics class, a Jewish Philosophy class, and American Government. I had intended to take a sculpture class instead of the Jewish Philosophy but it got cancelled.

Ceramics was fun. I thoroughly enjoyed that class, and made a few memorable pieces. My favorite was my final project. We had to make a piece that expressed an emotion. I was terrified when I first heard the assignment because I had no clue how to do this. I was reading a book on string theory, and in it was an illustration of what space would look like under a microscope. The word quirky popped into my head, and I had it. I would do quirkiness. Once I had my inspiration the ideas started to flow. I made a board, similar to a chess board. The outer edges of the board had squares on them like a chess board, but as I worked on the inner parts of the board the shapes became more complex. I carved simple orderly designs into the outer squares, and more complex disorganized ones as I neared the center. This was to represent the orderly way we present ourselves to the world, and the inner chaos we hide. Then I made 18 pieces each representing a different emotion such as joy, sadness, and excitement. Yes, I saw the irony, but I was on a roll. I chose the number 18 because it represents life in Judaism. The pieces were separate so you could move them around. On and off the board, in different places depending on whether you were outwardly expressing the emotion or keeping it inside you. I got an A in that class, and it wasn't easy to get an A in that class. The instructor knew most people took it as an easy out, so she was very strict with her grading. Only one student got an A+. I was in awe of that student. He was so incredibly creative. I had no idea how he came up with his ideas.

The Jewish Philosophy class was an interesting experience for me. I had studied Judaism extensively, including some Jewish Philosophy, but, this was the first time I was learning about it from a secular perspective. Most of the students were Jewish Americans and I did not relate to them at all. I ended up studying with a young Muslim woman from Pakistan. I had more in common with her than I did the American Jews, and I learned a lot about her culture.

I chose American Government because I had no idea how the American Government worked. I knew all the ins and outs of how the Israeli Government worked, but nothing about American Government. I felt that, if I was going to live in the US, I should understand how the government worked. So I learned about the checks and balances, the federalist papers, bill of rights, and constitutional amendments. The thing that had me most baffled was the electoral college. I still don't understand why that hasn't been abolished.

By my second semester at Rutgers, I had found a research assistant position with one of the Environmental professors. It wasn't a soil lab but there was a lot I could learn so I took it. A year later there was an opening in a soil lab and I got the job. Unfortunately, after about three months the professor told me he was low on funds, and since I was the last one in, I was the first one out.

A year later during a gym class I heard another student who worked in the soil lab talking about being fired from the lab. She had been caught stealing. I wondered if that was why I was let go so suddenly. Did she start stealing when I started working, and he assumed it was me? I don't know for sure but I suspect that's what happened. I wanted to go talk to the professor, but knew I wouldn't be able to get the words out. So I decided to just let it go. Even though I knew I wouldn't be able to speak under those conditions, I still didn't realize I had a speaking problem. After all, one could be rendered speechless. It seemed quite normal to me to have these bouts of mutism.

The science classes went well. I loved doing poster projects and term papers. I had left Hebrew U so early I never got to do any there. The reason I enjoyed them so much was that, as long as it was related to the class subject, I could pick something I wanted to learn more about. It was never an issue for team projects. I would pick the topic, do all the work, teach my teammates just enough for them to slide by, and get my A. I did try to give them part of the work, but always ended up doing everything myself. The professors knew I was doing all the work, but because I made sure my team knew enough to answer some basic questions I got away with it.

My most memorable poster session was related to climate change. I did a project predicting the effects of climate change on tree lines. Trees grow in areas that suit their needs. As the climate would be changing trees would start growing in different places, and others would take their place. I showed two scenarios, one with runaway climate change where all the permafrost melted and the soil organic matter in soil got consumed by soil bacteria releasing tons and tons of carbon dioxide and methane into the atmosphere. The other scenario was without runaway climate change. During the presentation portion of the session, we were required to walk around and ask other projects questions. My honed scientific skills were in full display, and I managed to ask everyone questions they couldn't answer. I knew, from the glaring looks I got, that when it was our turn they would be going for the jugular, so I made sure I was the one answering all the questions. They tried to trip me up, and failed. I was too well versed in the subject.

Looking back, I can see why they would think I was being obnoxious, even though I wasn't trying to be obnoxious. The class topic interested me, and being autistic I had done a very deep dive into it. I thought the questions I was asking were pertinent and interesting. My time at Hebrew U had taught me to go for the most difficult question. But if looks could kill that day, I'd be dead. The entire class hated me by the end of that day. For once I understand why. They were not graduate students, they were undergraduate students. Most of them wanted the degree to get a better paying job. Scientific inquiry was not ingrained in them the way it was in me. For them, all I was doing was making it harder for them to get their coveted grade point average and move on. For me, it was about digging as deep as I could into the subject, so we were in conflict.

As usual I managed to mess things up and forgot to take the psychology class I needed to graduate. Then I found out that in order to get any financial aid I had to be taking a minimum of 6 credits. Since I couldn't afford to pay for the class I would have to take an additional class to get the financial aid. I looked at my options and decided to take calc III and Introduction to Psychology the following fall semester. My advisor had told me that anything other than an arts or humanities class would work. There were easier choices than Calc III but as I have already mentioned, I tend to do better when I am challenged. It turned out to be an excellent choice because most of Calc III was a review of Calc I and Calc II with a few small additions. To do multivariable calculus you separated the terms for x, y, and z, or however many variables you were working with, did your calculations for each one separately, and then added them all up. Concepts I had struggled with in Calc I and II suddenly became clear to me. I was thrilled to find that as the professor explained some of them to us, I knew exactly where he was going with his explanations. I gained a much better understanding of calculus taking that class. Since I didn't study for any of the exams, I ended up with a B. But I didn't mind, understanding concepts was always more important to me than my grades.

The previous year, after losing the last research assistant position, I had started working off campus in lawn care. I started working for a small independent company, and I loved the job. The work was hard, really hard. Most days I would get home and be wiped out until the next day. But my boss treated us well, listened to our needs, and had our backs whenever a customer complained, so I worked as hard as I could for him. Unfortunately, it didn't last. Like with every other job I had, and would have, good things never lasted, and he decided to sell the company to a large corporate conglomerate. He did make sure we were taken care of though. Part of the sale agreement was that they hire his technicians to work for them.

The first few months weren't too bad. I was considered a rookie so there were some allowances made for me. But when I came back after the winter break, even though I had only worked there for two months, I was considered a seasoned worker and had to meet full quotas. It was expected that I already knew my area well enough to not need the breaks I had gotten the previous fall when I started working there. That would have been manageable, but, I kept getting sent to other people's areas where I didn't know roads. No allowances were made for that, I still had to meet the full daily quota for that area. Then, to make things worse, sales suddenly started going haywire. They were selling the cheapest package that was meant for lawns up to 1000 sq ft for lawns well over that. I think the largest I did was 16000 sq ft., most were around 7000 sq ft. But I was only getting the quota for 1000 sq ft. When I complained to my supervisor he told me there was nothing to be done about it. I was working 12 to 14 hours a day trying to meet my quota on the days I worked. Because I was still in school, I only worked 4 days a week, but I was working way more than full time hours, and only getting paid for 4 days of work.

When fall came around we had a new treatment to do. It was an expensive treatment that had to be done in addition to the regular treatments we were doing. At first I thought this would make the job easier, I could meet my quotas faster with this additional treatment. Alas this was not to be, even though the company charged four times as much for this additional treatment, none of that money counted towards our daily quota. I would now have to work twice as hard as I had been to meet my quota while the company raked in thousands more off my back each day. When I heard this I walked out and never went back.

Within a few weeks I got a job with another lawn care company. It was a franchise style company so it had more of the private feel to it. Their tree and shrub care technician had just left and I was hired to replace him. I was once again in a job I enjoyed, and happily worked as hard as I could for them because they were treating me well.

Chapter 11
Going No Contact

While I was working on my degree at Rutgers my mother's father died. He and L had been married for about 25 years by then. At the funeral one of her sons gave a eulogy calling him "the father." I was amazed at the amount of love and respect L's children had for my grandfather, and the contrast with my mother's hatred of L could not be more stark. But to me L was my grandmother. My mother's mother was still alive, but I had only seen her twice in my life, and never felt a connection with her. L on the other hand was always sweet and kind to me. L treated me like I was her own granddaughter and I felt like she was my real grandmother.

My grandfather had been in and out of the hospital for several years before he died. It was heartbreaking to watch him deteriorate. A part of me wishes I hadn't seen him during those last few years. Whenever he was in the hospital, whether it was for a few days, or months, L would go every morning and sit with him all day, going home only to sleep. Even in the end when he was in a coma for over six months, she sat with him all day, every day.

My grandfather left everything to L. I understood it. He loved her and wanted her to be comfortable. My mother on the other had a tantrum. She felt she deserved at least some of his money. When I pointed out to her how devoted L had been sitting with him every day for what added up to years my mother responded with, "Well, what else does she have to do with her life."

I was shocked by the callousness. But I couldn't respond. I had gone nonverbal. What I wanted to say was, "What about spending the time with her children, grandchildren, and great grandchildren?" Instead, I just walked away in despair.

My mother and her sister took L to court. I begged my mother not to do it. She said she was doing it for me. I told her I don't want the money. She went ahead and did it anyways. They did win a small portion of my grandfather's money and my mother crowed in triumph.

I felt sick when she gloated to me about it. A few months later L passed away.

My mother asked me to go to L's funeral with her. She wanted me there for moral support because L's children had accused her of causing their mother's death. I agreed with them. I saw how heartbroken L was after the funeral, she was in her late 80's and the last thing she needed was to deal with my mother's petty lawsuit. I decided to go to with her to the funeral. Not because I wanted to give her moral support, but because I wanted to go to L's funeral. I spent the whole time wanting to run over to her children and tell them I agreed with them, and that I had begged my mother not to sue her but I was too scared. I was afraid of how they would react to me, and even more afraid of my mother's reaction.

I did some soul searching and decided to make a final cut from my family. Over the years I had tried to rationalize my mother's behavior towards me. Someone had told me that parents always try to do their best with their children, so I kept trying to convince myself that her intentions were good. There was no way to spin what she had just done into good intentions. I couldn't stand being around her any more. There was no way to have a relationship with anyone else in my family without my mother butting in, she was too domineering, and did not have any respect for boundaries. I had no problem cutting them all out of my life, they had all done their share of nasty things to me over the years. I was better off without any of them. I have never regretted that decision.

PART II
Complex Post Traumatic Stress Disorder

Chapter 12
Heaven and Hell

Around the time I started working in lawn care my biological clock kicked in, and I suddenly wanted to have a baby more than anything. I was 40 years old and time was running out. I hadn't dated since my rape, but my maternal instincts got the better of me and I started dating again. The thought of going to a bar or parties to meet men was reprehensible to me, so I decided to try online dating. All my profiles started the same way "I'm different." I had known my whole life I was different, and had come to embrace it. Other people didn't. I did go out on a few dates but found American men to be very baffling. Something was wrong. In Israel I could hook any guy I wanted, suddenly men weren't interested in me and I didn't understand why.

In Israel there were very few rules, people tended to be very upfront and honest about what they wanted, and it was easy to navigate. In the US there are hundreds of little rules I knew nothing about and I didn't understand what was going wrong. Now I believe I got dismissed because I didn't know how to behave on a date. I was too open and authentic, and men found it off-putting. There is also the possibility that they were interpreting me in a nuanced way that put completely different meanings to what I said. But there was more to it. Children learn to socialize from their parents, being autistic made it harder for me to learn social skills, but not impossible. Being raised in an emotionally neglectful home made it even harder. Children raised in those kinds of environments are known to have more social struggles. Many learn over time from their peers, but I lacked the ability to do that so I was more stunted from a social engagement perspective than I ever realized until now. Then I met D, and my whole life changed.

I met D on a dating website in August 2005. Our first date lasted six hours, and it was hard to say goodbye after those six hours. After a few more dates though, I decided D was not for me. He already had two children, had had a vasectomy, and I was looking for someone to have a baby with. D reluctantly agreed to just being friends. We continued to see each other as friends but he continuously campaigned for himself insisting he could get a vasectomy reversal, and that we could make a relationship work. After about two months I finally agreed, and we went out to dinner to celebrate becoming a couple.

During dinner the waiter was a little too friendly with me for D, and he refused to leave a tip. At the time I thought it was cute that he was so jealous. Now I know it was a huge red flag. It was not the first red flag I dismissed. After I initially turned D down he wrote me a ten page letter explaining why I was wrong to turn him down as a boyfriend. In that letter he described all the abuse he had gone through as a child, and the fact that his father was in prison for attempted murder on his mother. But, he also told me that he had done a lot of therapy and dealt with his issues. He seemed like a good guy, and I liked him. I didn't want to judge him for his parents' actions, and after all, my childhood wasn't exactly abuse free, and I was fine. So I thought. So I ignored all the red flags and happily got more and more involved with him.

Things were wonderful between us, and after a few months we moved in together. It was my first time living with a man, and I liked it. D doted on me. He was everything I had always wanted. A few weeks after we moved in together he told me I was confusing him with my mixed signals. I was apparently still being standoffish and not totally letting him in, and he was finding it hard to progress in the relationship feeling so insecure about me. So I let all my walls down and was as open and loving with him as I could be, which made him do a double take because, as he put it, I became a totally different person. But he liked it.

Three months after we moved in together D suddenly asked me if it would be OK for him to visit his father in prison. I was slightly taken aback because he had told me he hadn't had any contact with his father in years, but, felt it wasn't my decision to make. I told him it was his decision, because it was his father and it wouldn't be fair for me to make the decision for him. D decided to renew his relationship with his father. Shortly after that, his adult daughter's car broke down and D decided to try and fix it at his father's property. There was a garage there, and he was very good at fixing cars so he thought he could do it there. The car had a blown head gasket which requires dismantling most of the motor to replace. It was not something he could do in our driveway. We drove there together. His daughter had gotten the car there, and the moment I walked onto the property I felt a chill. If anyone had told me before that moment that a building was evil I would have laughed at them. But, that building was evil. The longer I stayed there the more I felt it, and the longer we stayed there the darker D became. He was changing before my very eyes. By the time we left he was a different man. Like Dr. Jekyll and Mr. Hyde. On our way home he started verbally attacking me about something he had previously told me he loved about me. I was stunned, and very hurt. Over the years I had noticed that I sometimes overreact to things, so I had developed a habit of not responding to things immediately so I can think it over and decide whether there was a good reason for me to get upset. What I realize now is that these overreactions are driven by overwhelm. The next day, after giving the incident some thought, I confronted him about it in the evening when I picked him up from the train station. To my astonishment he started to cry. He apologized profusely for what he had done, promised to see his therapist, and promised it would never happen again.

D did go see his therapist, once. But over time he continued to verbally attack me. After each incident he would cry, make all the same promises, and then things would repeat. Each time he would go do one session with his therapist and claim he was fine now. Deep down I knew this was all wrong. Later, when I learned about the abuse cycle it all made sense to me. Then years later I learned about love bombing and realized that during our first six months together that's what he was doing. Not only was he love bombing me, but, he was learning about my deepest desires, and weaknesses to use against me later. As a result of the abuse cycle, I was going through overwhelm, meltdown, and shutdown cycles at an increasing rate. We broke up and got back together a few times. I constantly had one foot out the door but was never completely able to leave him. I kept thinking about the man I had met in August 2005, and our first six months together. I thought it was worth fighting for. I was also impeded by my insecurity over the fact that I sometimes overreact and was constantly second guessing myself. After a few months of this cycle, I stopped sleeping. My mental health was deteriorating fast, and I didn't know what to do. My brain was in a fog and I couldn't think. Every so often I would get a glimpse of the old D I had fallen in love with, and it gave me hope things would get better, if only... But that if only never came. I was slowly becoming totally psychotic from lack of sleep.

Perhaps the most troubling part of D's behavior that should have led me to just leave was the way he would change around other people. Whenever we were out with one of his friends he was suddenly attentive and caring. Not quite the D I had met in August 2005, but a close facsimile that left me confused because I didn't really know who this third person was. As soon as we got home and were alone, he would revert to his abusive self.

How I managed to get through those next few months on virtually no sleep without getting into a car accident is a mystery to me, but I did. I continued to work, was on the road all day, and somehow didn't crash. I did however develop my first "migraine." I was convinced it was a migraine because when I finally couldn't handle the pain any longer I spent two days in silence in my bedroom with blackout curtains drawn and the symptoms went away. But my despair was growing with every passing day. I would walk around people's yards treating the trees and bushes on their property crying nonstop. One kind elderly lady came out of her house and handed me $5 telling me things would get better.

Thanksgiving Day 2006 I snapped. D finally said something to me that made me suicidal. This was not the first time I had become suicidal, I had eaten some poison when I was in my twenties in a moment of despair over never fitting in anywhere. But I hadn't eaten enough so I woke up the next morning with a bad headache and after a few days all the symptoms disappeared. After that I decided that I had to accept myself for who I am even if no one else would. This time I tried to slash my wrists but the knife wasn't sharp enough, so I ran out, got into my car, and drove off. After rounding the first corner I saw a big pole, hit the accelerator and crashed into it. I knew I had to go somewhere and there was nowhere else to go. I wasn't wearing a seat belt but even though my car was totaled, I walked out without a scratch. I hid in some bushes for a while as the police cars drove by, then when things quieted down I went back to the house and in a rage started slashing D's furniture, because D had shown me over and over again that he cared about his things more than me, and I wanted to hurt him. In my psychotic fog I knew that hurting his furniture would hurt him more than anything I could do to myself. When the police showed up at the house the officer asked me a few questions, and took me to a hospital where I was admitted as a psych patient for attempted suicide. He also gave me a reckless driving ticket for driving my car into a pole out of despair.

While at the hospital I realized how stupid I had been. I should have taken D's car, and not mine was my first thought. Later I regretted the whole thing even though I knew that without D's constant mental abuse I would have never done it. I should have left him much earlier, but, by the time I fully realized that, my head was in such a fog from lack of sleep that I couldn't think. The week before my attempted suicide I contacted every person I thought was my friend asking for a place to stay for a few days so I could clear my head and think, and they all had reasons why I couldn't stay with them. If someone ever tells you they need a place to stay to clear their head please help them. If you can't let them into your house, help them get a hotel room, do something, please. If anyone had helped me when I asked for it, I might not have tried to take my life. I didn't bother calling my parents. I had just recently cut ties with them and I knew they wouldn't be helpful. When D started showing signs of abuse I was still talking to them so I confided in my mother, and she said, "That's what men are like, get used to it, your father is no better."

While I was mulling over my actions and what had driven me there a doctor came in and asked me a few questions. I think he was a psychiatrist because I was diagnosed with major depressive disorder, sent to a psych ward at a different hospital for two weeks, and put on anti-depressants. The antidepressants did nothing. The Ambien they were giving me did help me sleep.

I was looking out the window one day and saw D walking to the hospital and went into a full on meltdown. They sedated me and then put me on klonopin that only made me sleepy, it did not calm me down. The psychiatrist was so concerned over my behavior that he decided to have me transferred to a residential care facility after my two weeks were up.

Within a few days of arriving at the residential facility I developed another "migraine." There were no blackout curtains so I lay down on the floor with my face against the frame of my bed and put a pillow over my head to block out the light that was searing my brain. I hate having anything on my head but I was in so much pain I had to do it. Staff came in, a doctor came, said there was nothing wrong with me, and that I didn't have a migraine. He was right that I didn't have a migraine, he was wrong about there being nothing wrong with me. I was in severe sensory overload. At the time I was angry about them not believing I had a migraine. I was once again telling people I was in pain and being dismissed. Had they listened to me they might have dug deeper and realized I was autistic. There was no spectrum at the time but I could have been diagnosed with Aspergers. Between the light sensitivity, the meltdowns, and my constant issues with the food, all the signs were there, they just couldn't be bothered to connect the dots.

There is no way of knowing what my life outcomes would have been had I been diagnosed with autism fifteen years earlier. There are still a lot of stigmas surrounding even high masking autism, and back then it was worse. I do know for certain that I was robbed of agency. I was rendered incapable of making informed decisions, and of the ability to choose to tell someone, "I reacted that way, or, I am strggling with this because I am autistic." Besides being under-diagnosed, I believe I was misdiagnosed. I don't think I was suffering from major depressive disorder, I think I was in an autistic burnout.

***

Autistic burnout is something much discussed in the autistic community, but not recognized by much of the medical community, though that seems to be changing as more autistics talk about it. Autistic Burnout is significantly more severe than regular burnout. Symptoms can vary from autistic to autistic because we each have different sensory profiles, challenges, and talents. Severity can also vary from autistic burnout to autistic burnout within the same individual. As we get older the cumulative effects of our difficult lives and the strain of masking in order to fit in can make subsequent autistic burnouts worse. Some of the more common symptoms involve an increase of autistic traits. In my case, it was increased sensory sensitivity which is why I was suddenly developed migraines, increased difficulty handling change, increased volatility of my overwhelm, meltdown and shutdown cycles, loss of executive function and skills, which is why I couldn't think; loss of emotional regulation; increased difficulty with change; and suicidality. Another common symptom is depression, though I believe, at least in my case, it was more of a severe shut down than clinical depression. Now that I recognize shut down, I can see how shut down can be misread as depression. But I wonder if instead of being a chemical imbalance as is believed today, could depression be a form of shut down? Could depression be the mind regressing and partially shutting down because it can't handle everything, similar to the way the body will start sending blood to the body's core and not peripheral limbs when it gets too cold? I am convinced I do not suffer from clinical depression or major depressive disorder. What appears to be major depressive disorder in me is the very extreme end of the overwhelm, meltdown, shutdown cycle aka autistic burnout. Despite everything I have been through, I was a happy energetic person most of the time. I would go into shutdown when life became too overwhelming, and my system couldn't handle the stress anymore.

Masking is another much discussed topic in the autistic community. We mask in order to appear more allistic to allistics, in order to fit in and not be shunned by society. In order to do this, we learn certain behaviors, and suppress other much needed behaviors such as stimming. Some of us learn more socially acceptable forms of stimming that allow us to relieve stress while not alarming everyone else around us. People have an innate mistrust of "others," and not conforming to normal social constructs can have devastating effects on a person's ability to survive in society. Therefore, autistics are perpetually trying to perfect their mask in order to fit in. The problem is that in order to do this we need to ignore our needs, and do a lot of damage to ourselves in the process. Additionally, the need to mask, and hide our true nature is damaging. It leads to seeing yourself as bad. Masking on its own can lead to autistic burnout. Trying to come out as autistic can also lead to shunning, labeling, and being deemed as unfit for relationships, and work positions. At the moment, because of the way autistics are perceived, we are not safe whether we mask or drop our masks.

But doesn't everyone mask? Why would masking have such a profound effect on autistics mental health? That's because autistic masking is not the same as allistic masking. Imagine waking up tomorrow in a world where in order to be accepted by society you had to blink at specific intervals, and in a specific rotating sequence that repeats every ten minutes. How exhausted would you be having to integrate that kind of routine into your daily interactions? How long would it take for you to feel like interacting with other people wasn't worth the effort, because no matter how hard you tried you couldn't always manage that blinking task, and the actual socialization requirements? You would be making mistakes, and be shunned for your mistakes. How would you feel after years of having to incorporate that into your daily interactions, and being penalized for your mistakes? You may be thinking that this is ridiculous. How could anyone be expected to control their blinking that way, and why would anyone care how I blink? This is exactly how autistics feel about living in an allistic world with all its rules about proper eye contact, chit chat, saying how are you when you meet someone, reciprocity, not stimming, and more. These things as unnatural and inexplicable to us as having to blink a certain way at specific intervals would feel.

***

In addition to being in autistic burnout, I was developing Complex Post Traumatic Stress Disorder, CPTSD. However, in 2006, even though CPTSD was recognized in other western countries, CPTSD was not part of the DSM at that time, which made it impossible to get a CPTSD diagnosis. Many children who grow up in abusive and/or neglectful homes like the one I did develop CPTSD during their childhood. I believe I was spared because I had realized at such a young age that there was something not quite right about my family. When my mother stopped letting me visit our neighbor down the road I started emotionally distancing myself from my parents, later I started distancing myself from my brothers. Watching the dynamics of Perach's family solidified my suspicions. I did not buy into their judgements of me even though they were very hurtful. There was some damage to my psyche from not being able to have a good family bond, the nurturing of a mother, and parental unconditional love. I was never properly socialized, and never learned some important rules about engaging with other people, like how to set and enforce boundaries, but I did not have CPTSD. With D it was different. D was my knight in shining armor, and I loved him desperately. I wanted his love and approval more than anything. Like other children who never got what they needed from their parents, I was seeking that unconditional love I never got from my parents that every person yearns to experience. I know now that I will never experience it. Nor will the other countless children living in abusive and/or neglectful homes. This made it possible for D to take all the seeds my parents

98

had planted in my head such as, I'm never good enough, I'm unlovable, I'm a bad person, I'm defective, and make them bloom. My worst CPTSD trigger is not having my needs met, I'm unworthy.

In addition to attacking me for things he had originally said he loved about me, D played on my desire to have a baby, agreeing to it one day and backing down the next because, as he put it, I wouldn't be a good mother. Had he done it once and left it there I would have been OK. But he kept seesawing back and forth, becoming more and more hurtful each time. He would accuse me of being bi polar, or having borderline personality disorder, or that because my mother was a bad mother I would be a bad mother, and on and on. Interestingly, not once, did he suggest I was autistic. Each time I would go running to the internet to look up what he had called me, and was appalled at what he thought of me. I would also dismiss the accusations because the profiles were not anything like me. But each time he did it, the negative tropes my parents had planted in my brain grew a little more robust, and I went through another overwhelm, meltdown, and shutdown cycle.

There was also the never ending changes in demands. One day he would want things done one way, the next day he would want them done another way, so each day I was trying to follow what he had said the previous day but now it was wrong. I could never get anything right.

Abuse is hard on anyone, on an autistic, it's magnitudes more damaging because of the overwhelm, meltdown, shutdown cycles we go through that are so hard on our nervous system. In my case the CPTSD was working synergistically with the autism making my symptoms worse. The lack of sleep due to constant vigilance added its own dimensions to my struggles. My insomnia was driven by constant vigilance, and constant vigilance is a symptom of CPTSD.

In a way, I can now understand why D could have thought I was bipolar or had borderline personality disorder. Because of the autism my reactions were much stronger than an allistic person's would be. This is why so many autistic women get misdiagnosed with these disorders. My reactions were even more volatile than before because of the abuse cycle, the degradation of my mental health, and the loss of executive function that comes with autistic burnout. I suspect that his therapist was telling him these things because the accusations always came after he had a session with her. He wasn't going to her to deal with his issues, he was going to her to tell her the worst things about me and get ammunition against me. How she thought it was ethical for her to diagnose me to him is beyond my comprehension. She had become a very destructive third wheel in our relationship. Dozens of times I wanted to call her and say, "You win, you can have him, I give up."

When I was finally released from residential care I started picking up the pieces of my life. Thankfully my job was still waiting for me. Lawn care companies shut down for several months every winter, so I had not missed much work, and they wanted me back. I was the best tree and shrub care technician they had ever had. Spring came early that year so I was back to work within a few weeks doing early preventative treatments on the trees. It had to be done before they buds started opening so I was working long hours and glad for it.

I stayed in a creepy boarding house until I found a basement apartment I could afford. One of the first things I did was wean myself off the antidepressants. I had read up on how to safely get off antidepressants while in residential care, and started slowly lowering my dose until I felt it was safe to completely stop. The antidepressants had never had any effect on my mood anyways, which is another reason I believe I wasn't suffering from depression. They kept upping my dose because they weren't seeing the effects they wanted, and nothing worked. I did however start vomiting blood. Instead of lowering my dose, or stopping the antidepressants as I was constantly asking them to do, they started giving me medication to stop the bleeding in my stomach. Like so many autistics, I was being unnecessarily medicated to the point where my sensitive digestive system was being damaged. My digestive system has never fully recovered. After six weeks on anti-depressants, I was irreparably harmed. I had struggled with weight issues most of my life, mainly because of the emotional eating binges I would go through after every trauma. But, I was always able to lose the weight quickly once I came out of the subsequent shut down. Suddenly losing weight became nearly impossible, I was gaining weight more quickly, and my emotional eating binges became much more intense and prolonged. I also developed severe constipation that would take me over a decade to find a cure.

While I was in the boarding house I saw D a few times. We had semi repaired our relationship to the point where we were civil with each other, and he had Miri. He was living in his father's building, and even though I hated that building, I wanted to see Miri so I went there.

During one of the visits, he opened up to me, perhaps in an attempt to make me feel sorry for him and win me back. He told me that he hates himself, and that he loves me, so that when he hurt me, he was actually punishing himself because when I was hurting it hurt him. It was the most twisted and scariest thing anyone had ever said to me. It also told me that he was deliberately hurting me which was chilling, and it gave some insight into what had gone wrong in our relationship.

This is all my understanding and analysis of the sequence of events based on what I experienced, and things D had told me. A few days before deciding to renew his relationship with his father D had expressed a desire to go back to school and get his PhD. I told him I would support him in this endeavor. I didn't care if our life style would take a dive, I didn't need much, as long as we were together I would be happy. D was totally and completely overwhelmed by my response, and had never been happier than he was that night. Unfortunately, being so happy roused the self-hated he had worked so hard to suppress, and a need to sabotage his happiness took over. So, he decided to renew his relationship with his father to punish himself. While we were in his father's building all the memories of his father's abuse came back to him, overtook him, and he reverted back to the man he was before his therapy. I do believe that in his own way D loved me. Unfortunately, it quickly turned into a very abusive form of love that I couldn't handle. Instead of dealing with his demons as he kept promising, he kept looking for ways to hurt me, so that he could by proxy hurt himself.

I went back to online dating still hoping to find someone to have a child with, even though realistically it was very unlikely to happen, because I was obsessed with the desire to be a mother. I occasionally chatted with random men who had scant profiles and no picture, but nothing really stuck. One day, as I was chatting with one of these men, he revealed his identity. It was D. All the men I had been chatting with were D. He had been creating random profiles to stalk me online. But he begged me to hear him out, and I foolishly agreed. Despite everything I was still in love with the man I had met in August 2005, and even though I wanted nothing to do with what he had morphed into, I wasn't completely ready to let the D I had met in 2005 go. I also knew that if I didn't do this I would spend the rest of my life wondering "what if." D made me a series of promises, the most significant one was that he would never have contact with his father again. D was promising me everything I had been hoping for. I decided to give him one last chance. As I made this decision, I also promised myself that if things didn't work out this time, I would never give him another chance.

D moved out of his father's building and into an apartment of his own, he also got the vasectomy reversal, and proposed to me soon after that. I was feeling very hopeful and said yes. We made plans to move together. D had been accepted to a PhD program in another state and we were moving there together. I was sad to leave my job but I was looking forward to leaving the basement apartment I was renting because the landlady was batshit crazy. She was constantly banging on my door in the middle of the night to complain about the noise I was making fighting with D. Most of the time I was asleep, and she was waking me up. Some of the time I wasn't even home, we were at D's apartment. She would corner me when I got back and make her accusations. At no time did I ever have an argument with D in that basement apartment. We weren't having any arguments at all during that period. When I told her I was leaving she threatened to sue me for the rest of the years rent. I consulted with a renter protection agency and they advised me to make an effort to find a replacement, provide her with the names of the people who were interested in the place before I left, and that this would protect me from any lawsuits. But every time someone came to see the place my landlady would chase them off in a rage yelling that I had no right to be showing the apartment to anyone. I couldn't wait to get out. Since we were leaving the state, and I knew I would never get my deposit back I chose to not pay my last month's rent which led to more abuse from my landlady but I didn't really care by that point. She did in fact sue me but because she didn't have my social security number she couldn't collect. She had won by default because I never showed up, I was already in another state, and never even got the summons. I know about this because I saw her ad to rent the apartment online. It said in bold capital letters that anyone renting the apartment would have to provide a social security number. That was by far the worst experience I ever had renting.

We stayed in a motel until D bought a house and we moved in together. I started working at a local franchise of the same company I was working for in New Jersey, but it was a nightmare. In New Jersey all the pesticides they used said caution on them. At the new location many of the pesticides said warning which meant they were significantly more toxic. Additionally in New Jersey they were constantly telling me that my safety came first, and that if I couldn't safely spray something I shouldn't do it. My new employer emphasized that I had to spray everything regardless of the danger. I was getting covered with these dangerous pesticides almost daily and because of my education, and the work I had done in the entomology department, I knew just how dangerous this was. After two weeks I quit. I was feeling demoralized and went into a shut down from the bad treatment. I knew I needed to find another job but I just couldn't face it at that moment. I needed time to recover from the shut down but had no way of explaining any of this to D because I didn't understand it myself.

D's demeanor quickly changed. I knew immediately because Miri suddenly didn't want to be in the same room with him. Miri had always been very wary of him. When he wasn't being abusive she would tolerate him. When he was being abusive she didn't want to be anywhere near him. She knew from the beginning that he had a dark side, and I should have listened to her. A few days later I came across an envelope in his home office addressed to his father. When I confronted him about it he told me I had no right to tell him not to contact his father. I reminded him of his promise and he got angry. I saw the writing on the wall, and started moving all my things to the spare room on the other end of the house, and moving anything that was his out of that room. My dresser was in the bedroom we had been sharing and some of D's things were in it. I took his things out, placed them on the bed, and moved the dresser. D would later claim that I had thrown his things around in a rage. There were some of his things on the floor, but that was because he had dropped them there. D was constantly dropping his clothes on the floor. It's even possible that he had thrown his things off the bed in a rage himself. When I moved his television out of the spare room it slipped from my arms as I was placing it down. It only dropped a few inches but because it was so big and heavy, it was an old style TV, it made a loud noise when it hit the ground. D accused me of throwing it, but I could barely lift it how could I have thrown it? Then he shoved me, and when I called him out on shoving me he called the police. When the police arrived, he told them I was being violent, that I had tried to kill him in the past, that I was throwing things violently, and they just took his word for it. They told him to get a restraining order to get me out of the house. When D said I had tried to kill him in the past he was referring to my slashing his furniture. This was not the first time he claimed I was trying to kill him when I did that even though he wasn't even in the house at the time. When we got back together he apologized for saying it. About an hour after he stormed out two deputy sheriffs came to the door. When I explained to them what had actually happened they took me to a nearby safe house. I couldn't take Miri with me. I had to leave her behind.

Chapter 13
Homeless

Most of the other women at the safe house didn't like me. In fact, they downright hated me. I felt alienated and out of place, but I didn't know where else to go. The safe house got me in touch with an advocate who told me to ask for a counter restraining order against D. I went to the county and got the counter restraining order but asked them not to serve it. I was afraid for Miri. I was convinced that by now D had calmed down and would be wanting me back. If he knew I had placed a counter restraining order on him who knew what he would do to Miri.

I went to the library to use a computer and fill in a friend who lived in another state on what had happened. We had met on one of the dating sites. She was having her own problems and we were doing our best to support each other, or, so I thought. She sent me some emails D had sent her while I was in the hospital to use as ammunition during the trial. I was horrified by their content. I couldn't understand why D would want me back if this was what he thought of me. I also didn't understand why she hadn't shared them with me before. Had I seen them I probably would have never given D another chance. I became so distraught that I couldn't stay still. I started walking in the direction of the safe house. It was a few miles away and I knew my ride wouldn't be too long, I also knew I couldn't stay in that building. I was in meltdown, walking and crying uncontrollably at the double betrayal.

My ride showed up quickly, but, when I got back to the safe house I was in trouble for leaving the library and walking out on my own. They claimed I had put everyone in the safe house in danger by doing that and kicked me out. It made no sense to me. D didn't even know I was at the safe house so even if he saw me walking down the street in that direction how could I be putting anyone in danger. But they wouldn't listen to me. I suspect they had been looking for a reason to kick me out because the other women hated me so much. I tried to get into a neighboring cities safe house but they were full. I ended up in a homeless shelter for women where you were allowed to stay for up to three weeks while they helped you get housing and a job. Because I didn't have any children they weren't able to provide me with any services other than a bed and some meals. The meals were mostly things I couldn't eat. We had to leave during the day, we were expected to be out looking for work and I was. I had no luck the first few days. Then I stumbled on the state fair grounds. They were hiring people to clear out horse stalls that had been vacated. It was back breaking work, the manure was caked up to a foot deep in some places, and I was sore beyond belief at the end of every day, but I would take a pain pill, shower, go to bed, and wake up feeling refreshed and started all over again. I worked 10 to 12 hours a day. They were paying per stall and I was making decent money because I was working so hard. My boss started buying me lunches and taking me back to the homeless shelter every evening. I was clearing more stalls a day than any of the men. Those lunches were almost the only food I had each day. After two weeks I was able to get into the other safe house. I could stay there for three months. I felt like three months was enough time to get my life back together.

About two weeks after moving into the other safe house the work dried up and I had to find another job. I started working for the people who brought in the next set of horses cleaning stalls. Cleaning stalls is much easier than clearing out stalls and I wasn't sore every night doing that job. My first roommate at the new safe house was a drug addict. It was a nightmare being in the same room with her. After a week I managed to get a different roommate. This time it was recovering alcoholic. It wasn't ideal but it was tolerable. The food was at least as bad as the other places and I was reluctant to spend any of my money on food because I didn't know what the future held for me. I was buying a meal every other day, working very hard, and was constantly hungry. The safe house would have provided kosher meals for me if I wanted them, but they wouldn't accommodate my vegetarian lifestyle. Whenever there were vegetables they were smothered in butter which made me cry. I have never been able to eat butter, and they wouldn't put any aside for me before adding it. I did my best to find something I could eat there every day, but came up empty handed most of the time. I wasn't being difficult about the food, all autistics have very severe food issues. Mine aren't that bad compared to some others I have heard from. If an autistic cannot tolerate a food they cannot tolerate it. It's not a whim, it's not a preference, it's an intolerance we cannot overcome. I have tried to adjust to foods I can't eat multiple times, the more I try, the worse it gets. It's impossible to swallow intolerable food.

I noticed a trend at the safe house. The women fell into two categories, those who were actively trying to get their lives back together, and those who were just drifting. The ones who were putting in an effort had jobs and a place to live by the time their three months were up. The drifters ended up going to another shelter when their time was up. The saddest thing about the drifters was their children. At the time I didn't understand how a mother could sit and eat junk food all day instead of looking for work so she could support her family. Now I realize that I didn't know all of their circumstances, so how can I judge them. C/PTSD affects people in different ways, and maybe they had other mental health issues that were driving their behavior. I still feel sorry for those children, and wonder why there is no help for them.

With the help of a local woman who ran a support group for survivors of domestic abuse I found a job as an environmental scientist. It was a temporary position with the state environment department. The only problem was I didn't have a diploma. I had finished my coursework in fall 2005 but never submitted the paperwork to get my degree approved, so I technically had not graduated. I decided to swallow the little bit of pride I had left, and called Rutgers. I spoke with the dean, and when I explained my situation to him he immediately agreed to make an exception for me and granted me my graduation over the phone. I owe that man a huge debt of gratitude. Two days later my diploma and transcripts arrived in the mail, and I was able to secure the position. I would be working in the superfund oversight section. The position was for up to six months and I felt confident I could find another position within six months.

My court date arrived and as I suspected the first thing D said was that he wanted to have the restraining order dismissed. I refused to dismiss my counter restraining order. The look on his face when he found out about my counter told me I was right to not let him know. My advocate had advised me to not bring up the fact that D's father was in prison for attempted murder on his mother. She felt it would not work in my favor. I listened to her but regret it. I think things would have gone better for me if I had spoken up about it. When the judge agreed to a mutual restraining order for both of us, I couldn't go near him, and he couldn't go near me for six months, I wasn't satisfied. I knew that after the six months were over D would find me, stalk me, and do everything in his power to win me back. I wasn't convinced I would have the will power to say no. Despite everything I still loved him, at least, I still loved the D I had met in 2005. I asked the judge if after six months I could get another restraining order. The judge paused looked at me for a few moments, looked at some paperwork and said, "I can give you as much as five years."

I said, "I'll take it."

I knew that five years would send the message I wanted to convey, and that D would be out of my life for good. He would not wait for five years. D erupted but quickly settled back down knowing there was nothing he could do without making himself look bad. He was intelligent and self-preserving. I then asked the judge if I could go to the house to get my cat. I was very worried about her. I had found a foster home for her but couldn't go get her without permission from the judge. The judge agreed to my request and I went to get her with the woman who would be fostering her.

When I got to the house my fears were somewhat confirmed. We got there before D did so when he opened the garage door and Miri was in the garage surrounded by my things in a cage I knew she had been there the whole time. I grabbed her and ran. D was angrier than I had ever seen him but I didn't care. After that day, every time I would start thinking fondly of D, I would remind myself of how he had treated Miri. Even more than how he had treated me, this worked to subdue my fond feelings. I still had a lot to work through but seeing Miri caged like that helped me put things in perspective like nothing else did.

That dual personality was the hardest thing to deal with. In order to get over D I had to find a way to stop loving the man I had fallen in love with in 2005. It took time but I was eventually able to completely convince myself that the man I first met was a façade D used to entrap me, and that the abuser he turned into was the real D. I briefly spoke with a retired therapist at a synagogue. He helped me more in that half hour than any other therapist ever would until I met my current therapist. He explained to me that very few abusers ever stop being abusive even after years of therapy. He also told me that D was constantly trying to get me back, not because he loved me, but because he needed a victim. Even knowing all of that, it still took me a long time to completely get over D. I now know that growing up in an unloving home makes me much more susceptible to love bombing which is what abusers do to "hook" their victims. I still got away from my abuser within two years, which is a much shorter period than most abused women take. Part of it was the fact that I had no children, and I think my autism helped me break free sooner because I was able to rely more heavily on logic than emotions. But the emotions were still there which is why I continued to struggle for so long.

After many years I healed enough to be able to look at the whole thing more objectively, and accept that that our relationship was much more complicated than the black and white terms I created in order to stop loving D. I can now admit to myself that there was some truth to the man I met in 2005, and that he had legitimate feelings for me even though he was love bombing me because it was the only way he knew to go after a woman. I rarely succumb to the autistic black and white thinking autistics are believed to have. I think it's another one of those things that some autistics have, while others don't. But now I needed black and white thinking to deal with the tsunami of emotions that rushed over me every time D popped into my head, and I developed a deep hatred for him over the next few years. While I will never condone what he did to me, I understand that he was driven by self-hatred created by the negative tropes his parents had planted in him. I saw what his abuse did to me, I can only imagine what going through that, and much more as a child, had done to him. The hatred has been replaced by pity.

I had started dating again, and went out to dinner with the guy I was seeing that night to celebrate my freedom. He was probably the nicest kindest guy I have ever dated and I really liked him. Soon after that we went to a small local concert together and one of the songs brought me to tears. I was crying uncontrollably. My date told me I wasn't ready to be dating, and suggested we just be friends. I got angry because I saw it as a rejection. It would take me a few years to realize how right he was. I wish I could go back and just be friends with him. But feeling rejected I walked away from him.

It wasn't just that I was still struggling with my feelings for D. My CPTSD had gotten much worse. The combination of ASD and CPTSD wreaked havoc on me. The two conditions exacerbated each other. There are so many symptom overlaps between the two conditions, and they were acting like multipliers on each other. I sometimes wonder if

I would have ever developed autistic burnout if it wasn't for the CPTSD. I certainly never had it prior. Additionally, I was suddenly extremely anxious all the time. I had long since learned to manage my anxiety through inner dialogues. I have come to realize that some of the executive function I lose during autistic burnout is my coping skills. A few years ago, I was watching a podcast on getting over trauma and I was filled with despair because I had used those techniques, gotten better, and then come crashing down, over and over again, and I didn't understand why. I put in a comment about this, and well-meaning people started giving me patronizing advice that wasn't addressing my struggle. Those comments enraged me because I was trying so hard all the time. I knew they were wrong, I just didn't know why. Without knowing I was autistic there was no way for me to understand all the things I struggle with. If I sound like a broken record, it's because I am broken. Broken from dealing with a world I am not equipped to understand, and struggles I should have known about but didn't, because I didn't get a correct diagnosis from the professionals in time.

Living as an undiagnosed autistic had some challenges, but I had learned to cope with them and was even thriving to a degree. The addition of CPTSD changed everything for me because of the way the two conditions interact in me. I had no way of developing lasting coping mechanisms for this new situation. It's a combination that requires professional help, but I was unable to get the help without being properly diagnosed. Even if I had stayed in therapy at the time it would not have helped me because I was incorrectly diagnosed and under-diagnosed. The key to getting help for autism and CPTSD is having the correct diagnosis and finding the right therapist. It requires someone who knows enough about both conditions, and understands how they interact. Even then, a severe autistic burnout can take away all of those coping skills. I can get them back, but it takes time. Anywhere from several months to several years.

Every day I was away from D, I felt myself getting a little bit better, stronger, and less anxious. Over the next few years, I slowly started to feel like my old self, and through self-reflection, and inner dialogue eventually shrugged off the extreme anxiety and constant vigilance I had developed during my relationship with D. But I would never fully recover. I would continue to have emotional flashback from time to time, and autistic burnouts. It would take me twelve years to learn what an emotional flashback was. Emotional Flashbacks are a symptom of CPTSD. In regular PTSD you have flashbacks, scenes that pop into your head and take you back to your trauma. In CPTSD there is often no imagery, the flashback is occurring because emotions you had during your years of abuse get stirred up, and you are suddenly back in the abuse, except it's all in your head and you don't realize it because there is no imagery associated with it. This makes emotional flashbacks much more difficult to pin down and deal with. If you have ever seen someone flare up for reasons you don't understand, it is quite likely that person just experienced an emotional flashback. Their response probably wasn't to the situation they were in at that moment, but a past trauma memory.

What's interesting about my emotional flashbacks is that when I do occasionally get some imagery, I see my mother. Even though I didn't develop CPTSD during my childhood, when I did develop it, it encompassed my childhood.

Miri stayed in foster care while I was still in the safe house. It wasn't ideal but she was safe and I went to visit her as often as I could. Having me show up from time to time assured her that I hadn't abandoned her. Within a few weeks of started my new job I went to live with another woman I had met on one of the dating sites. I stayed with her for two months until I found a room I could afford. She never charged me any rent, and I am forever grateful to her for that period. My new landlady was a very nice woman who had a cat of her own and a small dog. I was quite happy there even though Miri resented having the other animals there. At least she had my room to herself.

I had left the safe house after two months. By that time, I had a roommate I got along with, and was relatively comfortable there. Even though I could have stayed for the third month, my conscience wouldn't let me. What if there was another woman who needed the space more than I did? Since I had found a place to go I felt it would be wrong to possibly put another woman in jeopardy by staying there. When I got my first paycheck from my job with the environment department I went to the safe house and gave them $200.00. They told me it wasn't necessary, that I didn't owe them anything for my stay. I told them that I knew this, that I wanted to give the money. They had saved my life and I wanted to pay it forward. For years I continued to make contributions both to them and the homeless shelter I had stayed in for two weeks.

Chapter 14
Rebounding

Because I was a temp my duties at the environment department were limited. I was put to work doing pre-CERCLA screenings that served to determine if there could be an issue that needed to be addressed at a site, and who would ultimately be responsible for the cost of the cleanup if there was the need for a cleanup. The most important thing I learned from that job was that having a degree did not mean you could do a job. For that job, and every subsequent job I have had since, there was a learning curve. College gave me some tools and some knowledge, but I could never walk into a position and hit the ground running. At best, I might be walking, usually I would be crawling for at least a few days. I learned a lot about reading environmental reports, and lab reports, and how to structure my own documents. I also learned how to do things in Word I never knew existed. Most importantly I became friendly with a coworker, B, from another section who would be my mentor for years until he left the state to work for a city. B knew water quality upside down and inside out. He headed the section that handled contaminated sites at the state level. No matter how busy he was, he always made time to talk to me about situations I needed help with, and I have unending respect for him.

The hardest thing for me was adjusting sitting at a desk all day. Between my years working with horses, and the lawn care positions I had spent most of my adult life working outdoors. There was the lab work, and the waitressing, but that wasn't sitting behind a desk all day, I was constantly on the run. My years working as a ticketing agent for the airlines was so long ago, I could barely remember it. It took some time for me to adjust to sitting at a desk all day, but I had no choice, so I did. After a while I started to really enjoy the work. It was like solving puzzles, and I love solving puzzles. That made adjusting to sitting at a desk much easier.

About a month after starting the position my section chief decided

I was ready to tackle a phase I report. Phase I reports were more in depth than a pre CERCLA screening, and significantly more challenging. It was like going from a 50 piece puzzle to a 1000 piece puzzle. The first phase I was assigned to work on was an incomplete report someone else had started but never finished because she died of cancer. I read what she had done and tried to finish it but it became more and more apparent that she was on the wrong track. It also failed to follow the format they had provided me with, but, I decided to not change that. Eventually, I had to abandon what she had been pursuing, and follow the evidence I was seeing. My section chief was not happy about this. She idolized the woman who had been the section chief before her and had stepped down when she got the cancer diagnosis. All I could conclude was that the cancer treatments she was on were affecting her judgement because she was clearly on the wrong track. Eventually my section chief accepted my conclusions though she still had a lot of things to teach me about writing a phase I. I was quite demoralized by how my first phase I had gone and was determined to do better.

My second phase I was a new site and I was able to follow the format they had provided me. Even though it still came back to me covered in corrections everyone was very pleased with me. They told me not to take the corrections personally, that everyone's reports went through the same rigorous review, and they all looked like that. It was part of the process. So I stopped worrying about reviews. Even the Bureau Chief stopped by to congratulate me on the job I had done on my second phase I. It was actually an embarrassing moment because I had popped a piece of chocolate into my mouth seconds before he walked in and had chocolate all over my mouth.

My most interesting Phase I was in a small town where there had been dozens of dry cleaners because of a shut down air force base. The dry cleaners went out of business but often their leaky underground tanks of PCE (Perchloro Ethylene, sometimes called Tetrachloro Ethylene) used in dry cleaning remained underground. That town seemed to have more PCE plumes than any other town in the state. What made this one interesting is that when I got it I was told the PCE was most likely coming from the active dry cleaner across the street. The data was telling me otherwise. Based on the concentration gradient I concluded that the plume was coming from a different direction, most likely a shut down dry cleaner that had been in operation years ago. I found two historic dry cleaners in the direction and vicinity I thought the contamination was coming from. I even went as far as finding old water quality reports from the transportation department that they had performed a few years prior when expanding the road. The reports showed a PCE plume with a gradient that matched the site I was investigating moving in my sites direction from the direction I had predicted. I couldn't say in a phase I where the source was because I lacked the evidence to give a conclusive answer without more testing, but I could say that it was more likely to be coming from the direction I thought it was coming from. I got a lot of pushback from my section chief but stood my ground on where I thought the contamination was coming from, and the report went to EPA with my opinion intact. About a year later they found the leaky underground PCE tank exactly where I predicted it would be, beneath one of the old dry cleaners I had found.

My job search was not going well. To make matters worse the cell phone I had from D, that the judge had ordered I could keep and that he should keep paying for got cut off. This meant that all the applications I had sent out with that phone number on it were no good. Most contact for an interview was made by phone. I decided it wasn't worth the hassle of going back to court, I would just get a new number for it and move on. I might even be able to get that same number back since it just went offline. When I got to the store the clerk informed me that the phone had been reported stolen. At that point I decided I had to go back to court. Reporting the phone stolen was a step too far. I ended up going back to court a third time to get my things. When I told the judge I was afraid to meet D at a neutral location to get my things she dismissed my fears. D had done a good job of being his most charming and she didn't think he was at all dangerous. I desperately wanted to tell her about D's father being in prison for attempted murder on his mother. I knew that this piece of information would most likely get her to change her mind. Unfortunately, I went mute and couldn't get anything more out. I couldn't even speak when she asked if there was anything left to discuss. She wanted our case closed out permanently. There was the matter of the expensive satellite internet system I had paid to have installed in D's house but I still couldn't speak so I said nothing. Outside the courtroom D and I agreed that he would put my things in a storage locker and leave the key at the main desk for me. Neither of us wanted to have to meet again. As

I had predicted getting a 5 year restraining order had told D he was never getting me back, and he was ready to move on.

I was relieved to have my things even though I didn't have the space for all of it and had to leave some of it in a different storage locker. There were some things in there I didn't want. Things D and I had bought together. I suppose he felt he was being honorable giving me some of those things. I ended up selling, donating, and giving them all away. I wanted nothing from my time with D. Not even the clothes I had bought while we were together, or any clothes he had particularly liked. Anything that reminded me of him had to go. One thing I never found was the rose painting from my last landlady in Israel. As much as I wanted that painting back, I felt it was not worth another day in court, so I sadly let it go. I do wonder if D kept in on purpose, I will never know.

I was getting interviews for permanent positions with the state, but no job offers. Out of desperation I called one interviewer back after getting the rejection letter to find out what I had done wrong. It was an entry level position and I had been so confident I would get it. I was choking back tears as I talked to her. She told me I hadn't done anything wrong there was just a more qualified applicant who got the position. I was starting to despair at ever getting another job. Soon after starting the temporary position, I got a call back from a big private contractor. It was for a position on an air force base in another state monitoring their groundwater. We set up a time for a phone interview. At the very beginning of the phone interview, I brought up the issue of my dual citizenship. Since this would be on an air force base I needed to be sure, before we went any farther, that this would not be an issue. The interviewer assured me it was not a problem. Soon after the phone interview I flew out for an in person interview at the air force base, all expenses paid, and a few weeks after that they offered me the position. There was one problem. I would have to give up my Israeli citizenship. I was upset because I had asked about this and had been told it was not a problem. Then I assessed my situation and decided I needed the work so I had to do this. I was sure I would be able to get it back later if I wanted to. So I called them and accepted the terms.

As sure as I was that I could handle giving up my dual citizenship, while I was on hold with the Israeli Embassy listening to old Israeli songs I started to realize this was not going to be so easy. When I spoke with the embassy I found out that if I gave up my Israeli citizenship I would never be able to get it back. I went into a meltdown. I printed out the paperwork and sat staring at it for hours crying. I finally realized I wouldn't be able to do this. I couldn't give up a piece of my identity. I had dual citizenship from birth. Even if I never went back to live in Israel, it was part of who I am. I finally called them again and told them I couldn't take the job. I must have been put on a blacklist because after that I never got a response from any private contractor I applied to. Knowing what I now know about the industry I understand it. Government jobs are what keeps these contractors in business, so they couldn't afford to have someone on their payroll who couldn't work at any government sites. At the time it was devastating. My six months were running out and I had no job to go to.

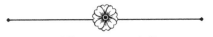

Chapter 15
The Health Inspector

I t was my last day and I was preparing to leave. Saying my goodbyes, struggling to contain my tears, and giving my unfinished files to other people to finish. I was feeling crushed that I had no job to go to. Maybe I could get on unemployment? I wasn't sure. At around noon my section chief popped in and told me to stop, that she was working on getting me an extension. I knew that extensions for temps were very rare so I didn't want to get my hopes up. I cleared out my desk and took my things to my car. By 3 PM I had finished doing everything I needed to do to leave, I was just waiting out the last two hours. At 4 PM my section chief came over beaming, she had gotten me the extension, I could stay for another three months. My relief and gratitude were through the roof. I scurried around getting my files back, and my things from my car, by 5 PM everything was back in place, and I was ready to come back the next day to give it my all.

A month after getting the extension I had a job offer for a permanent position with the state as an environmental health inspector. I would be regulating restaurants, private septic systems, and public swimming pools in a rural part of the state. That combination had me puzzled for weeks. I asked my coworkers but they had never bothered to even ponder the question. Once I learned the ins and outs of each set of regulations, I finally figured out why they had been lumped in together. They were all driven by microbiology. Restaurant food safety was mainly aimed at preventing food borne illnesses caused by microorganisms, septic systems were driven by microorganisms, and pool health was, at least partly, all about keeping the microbiology at bay.

I spent the majority of my first few months in training. Some of it in the classroom, and some of it going out with a seasoned inspector to learn about performing the job in the field. One of the trainings was to be certified to inspect existing unpermitted septic systems for registration, and my coworkers and division director were participating in that one with me. The training had to be repeated every few years. I was sitting right in front of the division director, and I fell asleep. I was incredibly embarrassed, but he never said anything to me. Maybe if I hadn't passed the test he would have, but I aced it. I had learned about water treatment in college and it included septic systems.

I was determined to be the inspector who hit the ground solo quicker than anyone else, and I succeeded. My first solo day was a Saturday. We were technically closed on Saturdays but health inspectors often worked Saturdays because of weekend events that needed to be monitored for compliance. Temporary food service stalls required constant inspections to keep the public safe. I was heading north to a high school where I knew they had a football game, and no one had applied for a food permit. I knew there had to be a concession stand, and I was going to catch them red handed.

Sure enough there was a concession stand at the football game. But I wasn't just looking for a score. I knew from my training, that a large part of my job was to educate. So I spent over an hour talking to the man who was running the concession stand about the need to get a permit and how food needed to be handled in order to keep the public safe. I could tell that he really hadn't meant to break any rules. He had apparently been doing this for quite a while and no one had told him he was doing anything wrong. So I wrote him a Notice of Violation with a warning. I didn't want to give him a fine. This would become my method of operation, I always issued warnings first time serving someone a notice of violation, warning them that if I ever had to issue them a second one it would include a fine. I never had to issue a notice of violation with a fine, and I issued a lot of notices of violation.

One of the facilities I had to inspect on an annual basis was the county jail kitchen. I had only been to a jail once when I accompanied D on one of his visits to see his father before things got really bad between us. It was an unsettling experience, and I was not looking forward to inspecting the county jails kitchen, but it had to be done. I walked up to the woman behind the Plexiglas who was processing visitors and showed her my credentials. She smiled and told me to come in. The door next to her window opened and I was let into the county jail offices. Someone was sent to get the deputy warden who would escort me to the kitchen. I waited nervously, and suddenly a big burly man showed up with a big smile on his face. "Hey, how are you doing, haven't seen you in a long time."

I had no idea where this man thought he knew me from but didn't want to ask. "I'm fine, how are you?"

We exchanged a few more pleasantries and he proceeded to escort me through automatic gates into the prison.

Just going through those gates made me feel claustrophobic, but I had a job to do. Once we got the kitchen and I started working I forgot about everything else. I found a lot of violations and we went back to the deputy warden's office to set up a schedule to get things fixed. As we were working out the schedule I suddenly realized where he knew me from. This was the man who had been running the concession stand at the football game the first day I was out on my own. I had written a notice of violation to the county jails deputy warden.

I couldn't get out of there fast enough. Back at the office I told my coworkers about the whole thing, and they laughed. They jokingly told me I needed to be very careful now because the last place I would want to end up is in that prison. Even though I knew they were joking, I also knew there was a ring of truth to what they were saying.

Working with the public was a challenge for me. Even though Autistics struggle with being told what to do, we love rules. Rules make life easier to navigate and we tend to follow them dogmatically. I still had to understand the reason behind every rule, and would often be explaining them to people to soften the blow of having to fix all the violations I had found. I knew this would have helped me, I don't know if this helped them but I did it anyways believing it was helping. Looking back, I wonder if I wasn't just annoying them with all my explanations. I was very regimented in how I performed my duties. Everyone had to be treated the same, and everyone wanted me to give them an exception.

There were two septic system contractors I worked with on a regular basis, and once they got used to my style of regulation and understood there was nothing personal about how I did things we got along just fine. They were good contractors and had no problem doing things by the book. Other contractors continued to try and get away with things and were constantly complaining about me to my Division Director. What bothered me the most was that each time my division director would automatically side with the contractor and not me. Upon further investigation he would find that I was correct, but he never stopped automatically siding with them. I always felt like he didn't have my back.

Besides my dogmatic thorough following of the rules I am also much more observant and thorough than other people are. I am not at all saying that the other inspectors weren't doing their job, just that I probably noticed things, and went into details others might not. It is well documented that many autistics are more thorough, and detail oriented than most allistics. This could create an illusion of being unnecessarily, or even egregiously, nitpicky. Of course, I lacked the awareness at the time that this could be going on, or the ability to explain this to anyone.

My observation powers were in full force the day we had a meeting with our district manager and liquid waste specialist. They worked out of a different office so we didn't have many meetings with them. I noticed that our liquid waste specialist was wearing a different ring, and it looked like it could be a wedding ring. Additionally he had just come back from vacation and I knew that the state his parents lived in had just passed gay marriage, and that he had been to visit them. I said nothing during the meeting. He was still partially in the closet because back then gay rights were still in their infancy and it was a very Catholic area. I had weaseled it out of him once when we were doing an inspection together. We had lots of time to chat during the drive there and back, and over time became quite chummy. We both had an off color sense of humor and would jokingly beat up on each other calling each other names I can't put in writing and laughing hysterically. After the meeting I asked the liquid waste specialist to review a septic plan I needed a second opinion on because I was once again being challenged by an irate contractor. As we reviewed the specifications I casually asked him if he had gotten married on his vacation. His jaw dropped and he took three steps backwards, stared at me for a minute then walked back and asked me how I knew. After I explained my reasoning he shook his head and said, "You are so damn observant."

The next day I decided to buy them a wedding gift. I figured they wouldn't have gotten many gifts because they weren't disclosing their lifestyle, and since I knew, I should get them a gift. The problem was what to get them? I didn't think they needed anything for the home because they had been living together for years. Buying something purely decorative didn't feel right. I was at a loss. So I went to the one person in my office I felt relatively comfortable with and asked him, "Let's say I have a purely platonic friendship with a man, and I want to buy him a present, what should I get him?"

"Beer," he responded. "Guys like beer."

I didn't think beer was appropriate so I asked for something more lasting.

"Tequila," he suggested.

"How about something nonalcoholic?" I suggested.

Next he suggested things like a pocket knife, a compass, a watch, nothing that would make a suitable wedding gift. Next I went online and it was close to Father's Day so they had a lot of Father's Day gifts. I fixated on a beer making kit. It was an activity they could do together, if it was successful they would have beer and guys liked beer, and if it failed they would have poop and our liquid waste specialist loved poop. He was always saying that his two favorite things in life were sex and poop. He wasn't in when I dropped off the gift but he called me the next day to thank me for the gift. He also asked me if I thought he was a lush, so I told him about the conversation with my coworker, and how I came to pick out the gift and he laughed. Then he told me he hates beer, but that his husband loved the gift. I think he threw that last part in to make me feel better.

I had similar issues with the restaurants. I never let things go, and people were getting very upset with me. But I was following the rules and stuck to my positions. Over time a lot of the restaurants improved, but there were always some problematic ones. I had my formula for dealing with problematic restaurants. I focused on high risk violations, and in my first year I went back over and over again until everything was corrected. I did this because I didn't know if any of the previous inspectors had been as thorough as I was, so I gave them the benefit of the doubt. In my second year I would show up with all of the previous years' reports, and if they had a repeat high risk violation from the previous year, I red tagged them. Red tagging was a warning to the public that the restaurant did not meet state safety standards and that they were eating there at their own risk. I red tagged six restaurants for repeat high risk violations in my second year, and two more because they didn't have a hand washing station in the kitchen. One of them had a plumbing issue, the other had taken it out because it was in their way. I was dumbfounded by this. They told me they were washing their hands in the bathroom. Yes, you had to wash your hands before leaving the bathroom, you had to wash them again when you got to the kitchen before you started handling food the public would be eating. I had no choice. This was an immediate red tag violation. Oddly enough, both those hand wash station incidents occurred on the same day.

Dealing with complaints was the most difficult, nerve racking, and entertaining part of the job. Most of the time when someone complained and we investigated, the person we were investigating would rat out someone else, usually the person they believed had turned them in. More often than not there was a real issue with the second property, sometimes an even bigger one. We called those situations twofers.

My most memorable twofer was one of the first ones I had. I had gotten a call about an overflowing septic tank. When I arrived, I saw clear signs that the tank had overflowed. I asked the homeowner when he last had the septic tank pumped out. He had never had the septic tank pumped out. It was supposed to be done about every five years to prevent solid buildup that could cause the tank to overflow. It was an easy fix. I wrote a notice of violation, and on it put the correction that he provide me with a receipt showing his tank had been pumped out within two weeks, and there would be no further action if he followed through.

The homeowner went ballistic and started taking me around the village showing me everything he thought could possibly be a violation I could write notice of violation for. Each time it was either nothing, or possibly a violation but outside of my jurisdiction. When I suggested he call another bureau he would respond with, "No I am not a snitch."

He finally took me to the house next to his where I found a violation I could address. The homeowner had grey water discharging directly to the surface which was a violation. Grey water had to be discharged underground where people could not come into direct contact with it because it often contained human pathogens. Grey water came from things like showers, bathroom sinks, and washing machines. Black water that came from toilets and kitchen sinks always had to go to an approved system. The man was elated that he had gotten someone else into trouble and went home satisfied. I went back to the office to get the Polaroid camera. We liked to use them because the photos could not be altered like digital ones could, and they had a time stamp on them. I wrote out the notice of violation, taped it to the front door, and took a few pictures as proof that I had left it there.

I was working late that evening finishing up my paperwork when I heard a commotion. "She wrote me a notice of violation."

Our office was closed so I walked out curious as to who was yelling, to find the man who cleaned our offices angrily waving my notice of violation in the air. I did feel bad for him but I had no idea who the house belonged to when I wrote the notice, and it wouldn't have mattered. A violation was a violation, no exceptions. What made the twofer so memorable was that the man who had shown me the violation, was his twin brother.

As regimented and dogmatic as I was with my approach to regulating, there were a handful of situations where I chose to look away. These were situations where it was clear there was no money to rectify the problem. At first I tried to get funding from the state. However, the fund the state had for these types of situations was too small to help all the people in need. All the money in that fund was constantly relegated to another district. One example of a case I chose look away was a disabled man whose wife had left him, and he was raising their four children on his own. He had inherited the property, but couldn't even afford to fix the house. I gave him a few things to do that would not cost anything. His septic system would still out of compliance, but it would keep the children safe. I placed his file at the bottom of my to do pile, and it stayed there.

The most disturbing complaint I dealt with was for cesspool in someone's yard. There was in fact a cesspool there, the stench was nauseating. I knocked on the door. It was the middle of the day and I wasn't expecting anyone to be home but it was part of the procedure. A rotund man came to the door wrapped in a crochet blanket and nothing else. I kept my eyes on a spot behind him the whole time we spoke, and was beyond relieved to get out of there. I never went back there alone.

I went to a lot of places during my two years working as a health inspector. I quickly learned that no matter how scary people looked, as long as I was respectful they never gave me any trouble. So I would always approach people with "excuse me sir" or "excuse me madam." That always softened their demeanor and the rest of the conversation would go well. I only got spooked once. I was driving to a complaint and there was a sign that said no trespassing. Those signs were ubiquitous in that part of the state and I normally ignored them. I wasn't a trespasser, I was on official state business. This sign was different. Someone had taken a black marker and written in big block letters "you will be shot." My instincts told me they meant it, so I drove back to town and went to the sheriff's office to get an escort. This was the only time I ever asked for an escort while doing my job. It took a while but a deputy sheriff finally came out to escort me. I could tell he was annoyed. After we were done at the property he turned to me and his demeanor had completely changed.

"You come ask for an escort anytime you need to," he told me. That property had spooked him too.

The hardest thing about dealing with complaints was finding the property. We would get directions like, "there's a big tree, and a doublewide, you can't miss it." Over time I learned that whenever someone would say "you can't miss it," I would get hopelessly lost, and never find it. I still tried my best, but it was like a stamp of doom. Occasionally I would ask a coworker to come with me in the hopes they could pinpoint the location but it rarely helped. We would also team up when one of us believed we were walking into a sticky situation that could end up in court and we wanted a witness. If one of us was behind on our food service inspections we would all go out to their area for a few days to help them catch up. This usually happened because of an illness in someone's family that required they take a lot of time off. For the most part we all worked well together, and yet, I never fit in.

The city the state fair was in had their own food service compliance team, so the state didn't have any inspectors there. When the state fair came around they would ask for volunteers to work the fair. Because it was on state property it was outside the jurisdiction of the city. I loved working the state fair. I didn't like the crowds but it got me away from my office, and I love new challenges. Most of the time.

When I was off duty whether it was at the state fair or in my territory I would tuck my credentials under my shirt. But I was always watching what was going on at any food service facility I was in. I decided to get lunch at a stall a coworker recommended. As I waited in line I noticed there was only one person working the stall. You had to have at least two people because the person handling the money should not be the person handling the food. Money is one of the dirtiest things people touch all day. I watched more closely and when

124

I saw this person take the money, take the next order, and then put on some gloves to start putting their order together I couldn't stay quiet any longer.

"Excuse me," I said loudly pulling out my credentials, "you can't do that."

What made me decide to intervene was the fact that after handling the money she didn't wash her hands before putting on the gloves. This was a very high risk violation and I had to intervene. If looks could kill I would have been dead. But the couple waiting in line behind me turned to me and said, "We're so glad you were in front of us."

There was a lot of driving and I had my own vehicle. It was a Ford Taurus and completely unsuitable for the terrain I was covering. Getting to a lot of my liquid waste inspections required going down dirt roads, many were barely roads, and occasionally there was no road at all. I kept taking that car places in never should have to go. It also had bad brakes, but when I took it to be fixed they couldn't find anything wrong with the brakes. One day I was responding to a complaint in a town that was over an hour's drive off the main road I needed to take to my next stop. But there was a sign for a town right next to my next stop so I decided to follow the sign in the hopes of saving some time. It didn't take me long to regret that decision. I was on a badly maintained twisty windy forest road with a sharp decline in a car with bad brakes, and no space to turn around so I had to keep going. It took me twice as long to get to my next stop as it would have driving back to the main road. One of my coworkers lived in the town the road led to, and when I told him what I had done he was in shock that I had been able to navigate a Ford Taurus through that road. Most people struggle to make it in a four wheel drive pickup truck.

One thing I noticed was that whenever I would go out to eat and would be telling the person I was with about my experiences regulating restaurants, my service got much better. I even got invited to see the kitchen of one of my favorite restaurants that was outside my area. I was a little wary of doing this because we had been told to never look at the kitchen or inspections of kitchens we liked eating at so we didn't spoil it for ourselves. I had also noticed a trend in my area. The more popular a restaurant was the worse the kitchen was. But in this case, it was a beautiful spotless kitchen, and everything was stored and handled perfectly.

The fact that I was Jewish was a sore point with my coworkers. They were all Catholic and they each tried at least once to convert me. I felt uncomfortable when we would go out to eat together. They would all say grace and I felt compelled to join hands with them for this, so after a while, I stopped going out to eat with them. There was a constant undercurrent of animosity that I did not quite understand until I had to take someone else's car to do my rounds. We each had our own vehicle and it was very rare to use someone else's but mine was being fixed and the other inspector was out for the day. I saw a bible in the passenger seat, and it was bookmarked. I was curious to see where it had been booked marked. It was a passage about Jews being responsible for Jesus' crucifixion. I knew I had to get out of there, and started applying to other jobs.

I started having trouble sleeping again, and was sinking fast. But finding a new job would take some time so I kept going until I couldn't. I thought I was slipping into another bout of major depression. I recognized some of the systems. Insomnia and excessive crying being the most prominent. I went to see a doctor to get sleeping pills, and after making me try several different ones including one she thought would be right for me because it was also an antidepressant, she finally prescribed Ambien for me and I was able to sleep. Of course, I wasn't heading down the path to major depressive disorder, I was heading down the path to another autistic burnout.

Swimming pools would open Memorial Day weekend, so we were all fully booked in the weeks leading up to Memorial Day weekend with our swimming pools. I didn't have that many in my area but was still booked solid the two weeks leading up to Memorial Day. Each swimming pool took about four hours, and I had a lot of driving between them. The area I covered was sparsely populated and very large. Most days I could only get one done, occasionally I got to two.

A few months prior I had received an application for a new food service. We had to respond to applications within an allotted time and I was careful to get back to the requester as quickly as I could. There were multiple issues that needed to be addressed before the permit could be approved. Months went by and I heard nothing from them. The week before Memorial Day as I was knee deep in getting my pools certified for the season the application returned to me with a note saying they wanted to open Memorial Day weekend. I called them and explained that I was already fully booked for the week and would not have a chance to review their amended application until the following week. According to the regulations I had 30 days to review and respond. They called my district manager and told him I was deliberately preventing them from opening up. I couldn't get my district manager to see that I was not deliberately being difficult. But he had gotten too many complaints about me, and even though none of them turned out to be valid, he insisted I was in the wrong, and insisted that I give them the food permit before Memorial Day weekend so they could open. I refused and handed in my resignation.

My district manager granted them the food permit. A year later I ran into him and he told me they had nothing but trouble from them since. There were problems with the amended application and they were refusing to fix anything. He also told me that after I left a lot of people started expressing how sorry they were I was gone, and what a good inspector I was. Of course, none of these people ever called while I was on the job because people only call to complain. It was gratifying to hear these things and to know that my district managers opinion of me had completely changed, but I had moved on.

I had not gotten any job offers when I handed in my resignation so I decided to become a full time student. I had started my master's degree a year earlier and was going part time. I could take out some student loans and go full time. I had been driving to the university for my classes twice a week, 90 miles each way, on top of all the driving I did for work. It was exhausting, and added to my burnout. I found a roommate situation in the city the University was located and made plans to move there.

Chapter 16
The Incident Response Coordinator

Two days before my resignation would take effect I got a job offer from the hazardous waste bureau. I was going to be the state's environmental incident response coordinator. IT was driven crazy because my old job was telling them to close me out, and my new job was telling them to expand my permissions. I would need access to things I never had access to in order to perform my new duties. The new job came with a hefty raise. They told me they had to get special permission to get me such a big raise but I was making so little at my previous job they had to do it to get me on par with what others in the bureau were making.

I managed to get out of the roommate situation because the landlord had not cleared the room I was supposed to move into. It was so full of junk I couldn't move in. Since that was part of our rental agreement I was able to nullify it. I found a place to rent in the city I would be working in, and cut back my classes to six credits. I would still be driving fifty miles each way to university but that was almost half the distance I had been driving before, and I had very little on the job driving. It was all much more manageable. My insomnia went away, I was feeling safe again. Autistic Burnout is believed to be driven by our inability to meet social norms and the need to constantly mask. But, I never went into autistic burnout until I developed CPTSD. I would get worn out, and burned out in the way an allistic person would, but I had learned to manage my anxieties so well that I rarely melted down. CPTSD and ASD work so well together that I was getting pushed into the overwhelm, meltdown, shutdown cycle much more than I had in the past. Every time I had an emotional flashback I would immediately start the cycle, and that would lead to autistic burnout. The worse I was being treated, the more frequent my emotional flashbacks became.

I was still in autistic burnout when I started my new job though, of course, I didn't realize it at the time. Now my decision to take things slower and not rush into all of my new positions requirements makes much more sense to me. I was rationalizing my inability to do this because I was in autistic burnout, and couldn't do it. It would take me a year to fully embrace my new position, no one was pressuring me. Autistic burnout can take anywhere from three months to a lifetime to recover from.

Complaints became a much bigger part of my daily responsibilities. I manned the department's complaints hotline and was in charge of going through the complaints and anonymous tips website where people could enter issues and didn't have to leave a name or contact number. Many of the complaints that had no contact information ended up getting dismissed because there wasn't enough information to go on. If there was contact information I always contacted them no matter how trivial the complaint was, or whether the environment department had the jurisdiction to do anything about it. I even called back a teenager who complained about how fish for sale were being treated in the pet section of a big box store to explain why we couldn't do anything about it. I felt that, since these people had taken the time to find the website, put in their complaint, and self-identify, I owed them the courtesy of letting them know someone had seen it, even if there was nothing I could do about it.

Because it was a department wide complaints hotline and database I received a much more varied variety of complaints. If they fell under the department's jurisdiction I would forward them to the appropriate bureau. I had an established contact person for each bureau. From that point it was no longer my concern. The complaints we had no jurisdiction over were much more eclectic and interesting. I took pride in how I handled those. When I first started the position I would spend hours on the phone tracking down whose jurisdiction the complaint would fall under. Over time I learned how to route most of the complaints and developed working relationships with at least one person in every federal and state agency, as well as many local ones. I always made sure I helped them as much as I could whenever they turned to me for assistance, so that they were always happy to help me with anything I needed. My most important working relationship was with the Department of Public Safety HAZMAT Coordinator.

Some of the complaints fell under no jurisdiction, and had to be handled civilly through the court system. I took extra time with these complaints. I had learned that in these cases the most important thing

I could do for these people was give them a sense that someone had heard them, and commiserated with them. I would sometimes spend as much as an hour talking to a complainant with a civil issue to ensure they felt heard.

I was able to master those kinds of work relationships because they were straightforward and easy to navigate. There were no hidden agendas or nuances I had to learn. Social situation were significantly more difficult for me and I have struggled with them my entire life. Growing up in a different culture exacerbated my difficulties.

Autistics often talk about having scripts for social situations. My experience has been that they do not work. I could find something that works in a specific situation, then try and use it in what I thought was the same type of situation and it would be a disaster. On the hand, for work situations my scripts worked, most of the time. It can be hard to navigate a different culture, trying to do this while autistic was magnitudes more challenging.

How I wrote my work emails was very telling. I would start by writing what I wanted to say. Something like, "I need the lab reports for site X." Then I would realize I couldn't send it with just that one sentence so I would start adding in "Dear Y," some platitude like, "it was good to see/speak with you earlier, as we discussed" or "I hope you are doing well" then end it with another platitude like "looking forward to hearing from you" and/or "have a great day/weekend." Somehow I could never write those things until I had written what was important to me which was "I need the lab reports for site X."

My second supervisor in the incident response coordinator position did complain to me that my responses to his inquiries for information were too short. He would email me a question and I would answer it, but he seemed to want more. I spent years trying to flesh out my email responses to include more information though I was never quite sure how much was enough. What did help me was asking him, and others, to always email requests for information so I could have the written request to review before sending my response. As I would review the request email I would suddenly realize, well, maybe I should include this, or that. I also spent more time fleshing out my responses with what was nonsense to me but was the "professional way to respond" aka with all the platitudes. However much I improved my emails, I always started with the sentence describing what I needed or the main point of my response and then fleshed it out.

Learning how to be "polite" in my professional emails was a little bit of an obsession of mine once I started working on it. This is very common with autistics, we can't do things halfway, it's all or nothing. But I could never translate it to social situations. I find idle chit chat incredibly annoying. I can't understand how people can just talk about, well, nothing, for hours.

Not only did I make sure to maintain an excellent relationship with the DPS HAZMAT Coordinator, I maintained a good relationship with all the district captains. They knew they could call me with anything and I would do everything I could to help them. Of course, this translated into me being able to ask state police to do a lot of things for us. Over the years I was there the number of inspectors we had dwindled due to budget cuts. For far away complaints I would often get a state police officer to go by the property and let me know if we needed to send out an inspector. Most of the time the answer was no, and I saved our inspectors a lot of wasted time driving too far out remote locations. I did ask the DPS HAZMAT coordinator once if I was overburdening them.

His response was, "If they have time to go for coffee and donuts they aren't overburdened."

I stopped worrying about it.

The first DPS HAZMAT Coordinator I worked with, G, became a friend. I called him by his first name and we would joke around a lot together. One day he called me about a situation in a small town down south. Firefighters had been called out to deal with a potential HAZMAT situation but they had no idea what the chalky yellow substance was. I asked G if they could HAZCAT it (hazard categorize through a series of field tests). G said they were too afraid to even try. He gave me the name and number of the lieutenant in charge of the situation. I called the lieutenant unsure of how I was going to help them, and got his voicemail. So I left him a message. When I got off the phone I had a message from G, the firefighters had figured out what the chalky yellow stuff was. I started laughing hysterically. When the lieutenant called me back I was still laughing. The chalky yellow stuff was the spent contents of a fire extinguisher. They figured it out when they found the emptied out fire extinguisher.

After G retired JF took over. I called to introduce myself and asked him how I should refer to him. Was it J or "Captain F" he responded coldly. I was a little taken aback, growing up in Israel I was used to an easy familiarity with everyone and G had never been that formal with me. That type of formality was foreign and difficult for me to navigate. After a few months Captain F thawed and eventually started signing his emails as J. At that point I knew the ice was broken. We were never quite as close G and I were, but it was a good working relationship. One day after he assisted me with something I sent back an email saying, "Thanks."

J responded with, "Just Thanks? Is that all?"

I knew he was being playful so I asked him if he wanted flowers. J responded with, "That would be great."

So I got on the internet and found what I thought was the biggest most beautiful picture of a bouquet of flowers, and sent it to him. J was thrilled with his flowers. After that I sent him flowers regularly, it always made him laugh.

Some complaints were very memorable. There was the woman who was convinced that a helicopter that had flown low over her house the previous night had dumped the contents of a 55 gallon drum on her roof. She heard it, and she wanted us to test her roof. I managed to not laugh out loud, and decided to take the time to walk her through the scenario and get her to understand there was no way she heard the helicopter dump the contents of a 55 gallon drum on her roof. I could not get through to her. Eventually, after about an hour, the line got disconnected on her end. I promise, I did not cut her off, but I didn't answer my phone when she called back. There was nothing we could do. Other than septic systems we did not get involved in issues related to private homes. The only reason we regulated private septic systems was because of the impact they could have on the states precious groundwater, and the population's health.

Because we never got involved with private matters I often ended up contacting someone from EPA to help us out in situations that warranted it. There was someone from EPA who was doing remediation work in the state. Most of the time I needed him to collect a jar of mercury from an elderly woman who had found the jar in her recently deceased husband's possessions. Some of these women had no ability to travel and that was when I would call the EPA guy. I had him driving all over the state collecting jars of mercury from elderly disabled women with no means of transportation. He would collect the jars and have them properly disposed of. I sometimes wondered how he got his remediation work done, but he never refused.

Then there was the man who found radioactive materials in the basement of a house he had just bought. Somehow it got missed during the walkthrough. At first I was worried. He told me it was potassium nitrate and yellowcake. Potassium nitrate is a fertilizer, but it's also highly explosive when it's concentrated, and comes into contact with water. Most of the time when a fertilizer plant explodes, it's because of the potassium nitrate. So he had an explosive and radioactive. The makings of a dirty bomb. Later he changed it to potassium di chloride which I knew couldn't be true because there is no such thing. Finally using CAMEO Chemicals and the description he gave me I determined it was most likely potassium di chromate. The yellowcake turned out to be uranium oxide which is much less radioactive than yellowcake because it doesn't contain all the daughter isotopes from the decay chain that are much more radioactive than uranium. The new homeowner was a nervous wreck about the whole thing. He had children and was concerned about residual radioactivity remaining in the house harming his children's health. I assured him this would not happen, there were no neutron emitters in the house, but he was so distraught I wasn't getting through to him. So I turned to humor. I told him that as long as he resisted the urge to snort, flavor any beverages, or season his food with the radioactive materials everything would be fine. He laughed and calmed down. I started calling people starting with my DPS HAZMAT friend. JF gave me a few options to try but none of them panned out. One of them was willing to take some of it but not all of it. That wouldn't solve the problem. Next I called my EPA contact who immediately agreed to remove and properly dispose of the radioactive materials. He also found out by talking to previous owner who was a widow, that her husband was a jeweler. Those were leftover materials from decades earlier when jewelers used these types of chemicals to color jewelry.

Another memorable complaint came from the cabinet secretary's office. His administrative assistant called me and told me she was transferring a call to me, and that I should call her back when I was done. On the other end was an elderly woman who started telling me that ever since the national guard had moved in next door to her she had been having health problems due to their illicit activities. I asked her if she had been to see a doctor. Most of the time people would respond no, and I could tell them to go see a doctor and call back if the doctor found anything related to their complaint. They never called back.

She replied, "Yes but the doctor can't find anything wrong with me."

I had to bite my tongue because the thought that entered my head was, "Lady, you went to the wrong kind of doctor."

But I managed to remain calm and sound concerned. I did my best to commiserate with her while explaining that there was nothing I could do because it didn't fall under our jurisdiction but she wouldn't let it go. Finally out of desperation to get her off the phone without hanging up on her I gave her a homeland security complaints website and told her to lodge her complaint there. When I finally got her off the phone I called the cabinet secretary's administrative assistant back. What she wanted to say to me was, "Was that lady a fruitcake or what?" The funniest thing about the whole thing is that there is no national guard in the city she lives in.

Then there was the dead body incident. A state police captain called me. Someone had decided to commit suicide by eating prairie dog poisoning. Then he had regrets and called 911. He was rushed to the hospital but it was too late. They induced vomiting, and he vomited all over the ER and died. The problem was that it was old prairie dog poisoning and it contained aluminum phosphine that converted into phosphine gas in his body. Phosphine gas is highly toxic and they couldn't release the body to his family until it was exuding phosphine gas at a low enough concentration to not pose a threat. The state police captain wanted to know if we could help with monitoring the level of gas the body was exuding. I told him I would look into it and called my air quality bureau contact who couldn't believe what he was hearing. After that, every time I called him, I would start with, "No dead bodies today."

The scariest incident I dealt with was a call from a science teacher who was working in a small town where they had one school building that housed K through 12. She had been going through the chemical inventory and found a one lb. bag of 99% pure benzoyl peroxide that had been sitting around for at least twenty years. She had been working there for twenty years and she knew she never brought it in. You may be familiar with benzoyl peroxide as the active ingredient in acne treatments. Those products contain very low concentrations of benzoyl peroxide, generally about 3% which is completely innocuous. But in concentrated powder form benzoyl peroxide is used as rocket fuel, is highly reactive, and the longer it sits the more unstable it gets.

Highly concentrated benzoyl peroxide is capable of exploding for no reason. State police bomb squad refused to deal with it. I didn't sleep for two days until an air force EOD went in, retrieved it, took it to a safe spot and detonated it. The entire town shook. Had it blown it would have easily taken down the entire K through 12 building. Thankfully no one got hurt.

Chapter 17
Emergency Response

A ll those incidents were spread out over several years. Most complaints were much less entertaining and/or eventful, and I had other duties. One of them was the departments emergency response. It wasn't glamorous at all. Emergency response is boring, boring, boring, boring, a few minutes or an hour of excitement, then back to boring. But it did have its moments.

You may be wondering how dealing with all this diversity of complaints, and multiple duties felt to an autistic. Personally, I loved it. It was like having new puzzles to solve all the time, and the more challenging a puzzle is, the more fun it is. The only time I struggle with multiple work assignments is when I am in autistic burnout, most likely because of the loss of executive function.

My favorite emergency response story is from my first month on the job. It was fire season, and an elderly gentleman who was renting a home on a piece of property that was part of an old mine called state police and told them there were sticks of dynamite and drums of cyanide in an old shed behind the house he was renting, and the fire was encroaching. State police immediately drove over there and searched the shed. They didn't find any dynamite but they did find four drums marked cyanide. Since I was so new they didn't even know I had been hired, so they called my supervisor who consulted with EPA, and together they determined the state could get someone out there quicker. So we sent a contractor out there to retrieve the drums and properly dispose on them. The firefighters had said they would walk away from the fire if it got too close to the shed, and I don't blame them, so time was of the essence.

The contractor decided to check the contents of the drums before removing them from the premises. Something didn't feel right when they started to move them. They put on their PPE (personal protective equipment) and opened the first drum. It had a big bag of rice in it. They opened the second drum. It had a big bag of beans in it. The third drum had some old traps in it, and the fourth was empty. The contractor still removed the drums and had them properly disposed of so they wouldn't wreak any more havoc down the road. The elderly gentleman walked up, saw the rice and beans and said, "Oh yes, I put that there." I can only surmise he was suffering from dementia. Still, the state had just spent several thousand dollars on some rice and beans.

Another part of my position was handling spill response. It was mostly road related spills because most industry had ground water quality bureau, and/or surface water quality bureau permits, any spills related to those were handled by the permitter as they had special conditions for spill response built into their permits. Most of the time it was a truck accident, and the trucks saddlebags got damaged and the diesel spilled. Sometimes it was more than that but even a saddle bag release could be interesting even though most weren't.

My most memorable saddlebag release incident was one down south. The driver called it in but claimed there was no clean up necessary because all the diesel and landed on a (magical) boulder that contained the entire release. He didn't say magical, I am saying magical because it was obviously a made up story.

Some other memorable ones were, the truck driver who did a nose dive of about thirty feet into a river and walked out without a scratch. The two trucks out in the middle of nowhere on an air force base who collided head on, the truck driver who got lost and was so disoriented he drove right into an artificial lake. I asked, and he was not drunk or high. My favorite truck accident that wasn't just saddle bags was the truck carrying beef, and the truck carrying lighter fluid that collided.

No one got hurt in any of the above incidents which is why I can laugh about them. But tragedy would occasionally strike. There were times when the truck driver didn't make it and those were tragic. The most memorable one was the truck carrying 6,000 gallons of gasoline and 1,000 gallons of diesel who went too fast over a mountain pass just past the state border and his cab got crushed when he rolled into the mountainside. That was also the biggest release I ever dealt with. It was such a remote place, and state police had the road blocked off. The truck that was going to salvage what it could from the destroyed truck couldn't get through and it all released to the environment. It became an even bigger problem because the trucking company tried to cut corners and had the contractor only working eight hours a day and only on weekdays. Had it only been diesel it would have been fine to go slow. But gasoline with MTBE in it (it replaced lead in gasoline) moves very quickly to groundwater. By cutting corners they ended up having to pay significantly more over the years for ground water remediation and monitoring. At the point it hit groundwater the incident got taken over by the ground water quality bureau.

Meth lab clean ups was the last thing I had to cover. There was nothing amusing about meth labs, they were pure tragedy. But I did get to go on a meth lab raid with a local police department. I had to stay far back in the car with the lieutenant who was the incident response commander, so I didn't see much. But I learned a lot about meth addiction from the lieutenant and it's not a drug you want to mess with ever.

I struggled when my first supervisor left because I did not get along at all with my second supervisor. My biggest problem with him was that he started demanding I release information I knew I shouldn't be releasing.

The complaints database I managed was created for internal use only, and was meant to help track complaints and incidents, and transfer them from bureau to bureau as needed. My second supervisor decided it should be included In IPRA requests. Even worse I was instructed to provide the information to data sellers. They would put on their request that they wanted the information for a phase I investigation but their website showed clearly that they sold data. I pushed back as hard as I could but got denied at every turn.

The biggest problem I had with providing the information was that people were entering private information into that database believing it to be confidential, and we were now violating that trust. I kept asking to have a warning placed that the information they were entering was not confidential and eventually they did put one there, but all the entries before that warning was put in were not aware the information was now open to the public. There were a lot of other problems with sharing the database information such as, it often didn't say if a complaint ended up being valid or not. I made a fuss each time I had to do one and was told I would be reprimanded and in risk of losing my job if I didn't do it. Each time I sent the information requested to my supervisor I would write in the email that I was doing this under protest, and I started having trouble sleeping again.

My third supervisor was worse. She started demanding that I change how I do everything. It was more than just being asked to create change that creates blocks in my brain. When I start a new position I am extremely insecure, and I dislike being ordered what to do. In order to learn my position I ask questions, lots and lots of questions. That way I learn what I need to learn without having to be ordered what to do. I am simply getting answers to my questions, and that is something my brain handles well. When I can't get the answers I need from my supervisor I look for answers in other places. For this particular position I would mostly turn to B. Even though I was in the hazardous waste bureau, the regulations I was working with were mainly ground water regulations, occasionally solid waste regulations, and from time to time hazardous waste regulations. I had my go to person in solid waste, and when I had a hazardous waste question I would ask my supervisor, or one of the hazardous waste regulators. I had spent years honing my knowledge base, my understanding of all the regulations, and perfecting how I approach things. I had developed ways of doing things that worked well for my brain. Suddenly someone who doesn't know me at all is telling me to change everything without even sitting down to talk to me about what I'm doing. The only explanation I got was that this was how she wanted things done. The message I was getting was that I wasn't doing a good enough job. It was insulting, demoralizing and untenable. What I didn't understand at the time was that I was in a mild autistic burnout from the way my previous supervisor handled the database IPRA requests which made handling change much harder to deal with. Added to that was her demand that I get back on the emergency on call rotation. My explanations of why I had stopped fell on deaf ears. My inability to manage two weeks with no sleep didn't matter to her. I had been on the rotation for the first three years but was getting so stressed by it that I couldn't sleep while I was on the on call duty. The lack of sleep was so negatively impacting my ability to function, that even though I really wanted the extra pay, I removed myself from the rotation. To make matters worse I realize now that I was already in an autistic burnout which made change harder for me to handle. I kept refusing, found another job, and quit. I handed in my resignation three days before starting my new job, in the letter I wrote that I would be using my annual leave during the next two weeks and that this was my last day in the office. That last day was also the day we did our 8 hour HAZWOPER refresher. I handed in the letter at 4 PM that day. It was as passive aggressive as I could get. I was angry.

Chapter 18
Unemployment

My next job was with a city, I decided to make use of my masters coursework and do something related to water. I didn't last long there. I was laid off after a few weeks. At the time I knew I was being misunderstood and accused of saying things I hadn't said. What I didn't understand was that I needed to change my approach. I was no longer a state regulator and that change in status required some changes in how I approached things. I just didn't understand that at the time.

Because I was laid off I was able to get unemployment. I was renting a room in someone's home so I was able to live off the money I was getting from unemployment. I spent some time every day looking for work but wasn't getting any replies. I decided to use the time I had to improve my fitness. In the back of my mind, I was thinking that if worst came to worst I could apply to become a police officer. I had enjoyed working with them, why not become one of them.

My last position with the state environment department was in an area that was perfect for hiking. I joined a hiking club and started learning all the routes. On one of the hiking trips one of the women started grilling me about my weight issues, telling me I needed some sort of weird therapy to figure out what was causing my weight problem. She said there was clearly something wrong with me. I got upset and started looking for another hiking group, but never found a hiking group I felt comfortable in. Then I came across a backpacking group and they were doing a trip that seemed reasonable to me from the description. I start training for it weighing down my hiking pack with water bottles and books and going for hikes I thought would simulate the type of terrain I would be going through based on the description. The trip leader cancelled at the last minute but a few of us decided to go anyways. One of them had all the coordinates downloaded into his GPS, we would be able to find the off trail lake.

I learned that the person who posted the description did not know the difference between elevation gain and total elevation gain. The description said total elevation gain 1600 ft, it was in fact around 3500 ft. On top of that we did a fair amount of meandering trying to find the lake, so we ended up doing closer to 4000 ft. But the lake was so beautiful, and being able to wake up there and soak in the beauty through different times of the day was amazing. I was hooked. My feet were hurting, along with every muscle in my body, but I wanted more. I invested in some good backpacking gear and became an avid backpacker.

During my year on unemployment, I went on 13 backpacking trips. Most of them were multi night trips so I spent on average 3 nights a week in a tent that summer. During one of the earlier trips, I injured myself. I am not totally sure when it happened but as we were packing out there was a pain in my right hip that was getting worse and worse. The pain started radiating up and down my right side. By the time I got to the last fork my entire right side was on fire. Knowing I didn't have far left to go I started counting my steps to distract myself from the pain. As soon as I got to my car and took the pack off it started to feel better so I didn't think it was anything serious. Over the next few weeks, I would dance and exercise, each time the pain would flare up but go away after I let it rest for a few days. I toyed with the idea of going to see a doctor but was already so traumatized by doctors telling me there was nothing wrong with me when I was in pain that I didn't want to. I finally decided to ask my chiropractor to check it for me when I went on my monthly visit. The chiropractor told me my leg wasn't in my hip socket. He pushed my leg back in and I continued to see him twice a week for about two months until I was sure my leg was firmly back in place.

There was still some residual pain but the chiropractor told me it had to be soft tissue related because from a skeletal point of view I was fine. Massages didn't help so I started experimenting with different exercise moves until I found one that worked and within a few weeks of finding the right exercise move I was pain free again. Then I went on another backpacking trip and somehow found myself with a group that was going in circles. I was familiar with where we were going, and I kept telling them where we needed to go but they wouldn't listen. My hip started to hurt again, and I was getting very overwhelmed by the pain and their unwillingness to listen to me. I finally recognized a landmark and decided to climb up the side of the mountain to get to the correct trail. By the time I arrived at the lake I was totally exhausted. I had to lay down for about an hour before I was able to start pitching my tent. Normally I would do that as soon as I got to the camp site.

That evening the guy who had been leading us in circles started teasing me and I blew up at him. But everyone else was taking his side saying I was making a big deal out of nothing. I was furious. They didn't know how much pain I was in. But instead of being able to get anyone to see my point I alienated everyone.

Growing up I was constantly told that I had two left feet, no sense of rhythm, and that I would never be able to dance. Yes, that was my parents. Because of their constant criticism whenever I would be at a dance I would refuse every invitation to dance saying, "I can't dance."

I was in fact a very clumsy child because of my vestibular sensory issues. But these things can be improved on, and through my years of horseback riding my balance and control had improved greatly. I briefly dated a man in New Jersey who was into competitive ballroom dancing and he taught me the waltz box step in his living room and told me there was nothing wrong with my feet or rhythm. Then he did a tango with me and I knew I wanted to do this someday. The relationship didn't last, but that memory of dancing did. Soon after that I met D and my dancing years got delayed. We did talk about taking dance lessons together but it never happened, and I am glad for that. Dancing would have been tainted by memories of his abuse.

For my 46th birthday I bought myself a series of dance lessons. I was so clumsy at the beginning it was comical, but through perseverance I improved. I couldn't afford many lessons, I was paying back $40,000 in student loans from both my degrees, but I went to every social dance I could get to, and bought every package deal I could find. I wasn't just doing I ballroom. I got into the East Coast Swing/Lindy Hop scene and Blues dancing. Every style of dance I learned added dimensions to my dancing overall. I did weekend workshops that gave a lot of lessons for relatively little cost. I danced so much that I developed shin splints. Since I had never had shin splints before I didn't know why I was in pain, so I kept going until I could barely walk from the pain. I tried acupuncture, massages, yoga, water aerobics, and nothing worked until I tried compression socks. After that I was more careful, and wore compression socks whenever

142

I started to feel a twinge in my shins.

I met Mayim Bialik at one of the Blues workshops. She was an experienced dancer, knew how to lead, and was kind enough to dance with me even though I was a beginner. I couldn't keep up the Blues dancing for very long. Their dances would start at 11 PM, things didn't really start happening until midnight, which meant I rarely left before 1 PM, got home at 2 PM. It was unsustainable, and there was a man there who was making me uncomfortable. But, for the most part, I enjoyed my time Blues dancing.

Two years after I started dancing I decided to learn how to lead. The Saturday night Swing Dance I regularly attended had an introductory class before each dance started. It was always the same few moves so it was a great place to start. The first time I tried to lead I felt like my brain was frozen. My body kept wanting to go back to follow steps and follow arm positioning. I took that class about twenty times until I felt ready to try something else. Over time I learned quite a few Swing leads, and even won a first place and a second place in two local Swing competitions as a lead. I also branched out a little into Waltz, Rumba, Cha Cha, and Nightclub. No matter how good I got at leading I always felt it was much harder than following, but it did allow me to be out on the dance floor more. The most fun I would have leading was dancing with a partner who knew both lead and follow, and we would do switch offs. They would lead for about 30 seconds, then I would lead for about 30 seconds, and back and forth we would go until the song was over.

During my year on unemployment, I started taking Israeli Folk dancing classes at the Jewish Community Center. The classes were taught by a young medical resident. I had taken a few lessons while in Israel but would get confused all the time on which way to turn so I stopped. I had to go the United States to learn Israeli dancing from a guy from Brazil. We even did a small performance for the ballroom club.

Through all of this something was going on that I was somewhat aware of, but, never said anything to anyone about it because I had no proof. The man who had made me uncomfortable Blues dancing had started showing up at other dances, and people started shunning me. I suspected he was bad mouthing me because I had turned him down and would not dance with him anymore. The thought of dancing with him again made my skin crawl. What I didn't realize at the time was that my subconscious was most likely equating him with N. Because he wasn't accepting my cues of avoiding him and constantly moving to the other side of the room, and kept trying to approach me. I felt threatened and avoided him with even more resolve.

Eventually, I was at a live swing music event at a hotel lobby where people from various dance disciplines had shown up. People were giving me strange looks. At one point two women from the ballroom club walked over to me and sat down. They pointed at the man and said, "He is going around telling everyone you won't dance with him because he is a beginner."

I told them the real reason and they 100% sided with me. No matter what, if a man makes a woman uncomfortable, she has the right to avoid dancing with him. They also knew that I often dance with beginners at the ballroom dances so they were suspicious of his claims which is why they came to talk to me. A few weeks later he showed up at one of the ballroom clubs dances. I was appalled and unsure what to do. The two women I had spoken to looked at me, then walked over to the club chairperson and talked to her, presumably about that man and our conversation at the hotel. The chairperson went over to the man and talked to him. He left and never came back. I had always felt that the ballroom group was the most supportive and accepting, and this confirmed it even more for me. No one else was willing to hear me out, I did try after that.

Winter came along and there was no more backpacking. I was in a new area, was unfamiliar with the trails, and fed up with hiking groups. I decided to start running. I would need to run two miles to get into the police academy. It was a daunting task. I had never been able to run 100 meters, but I was determined. I did some research on how to train for a 5k, and started setting out each morning to do what I could. The research I did suggested using a timer but I found counting easier. I started with 70 jog strides, then 80, then 90. Over time I started adding in 50 then 100 then 150 strides. Eventually I was able to add ¼ mile to my next run. This took over a year but I became a decent runner, and even entered a few 5k races, placing second for my age group in one of them. Then the chest colds started and I had to stop running. Every few months I would start running again but when I got to about ¾ of a mile the chest cold would come back. There was no way I could get into the police academy if I couldn't run. In hindsight this was a good thing. I don't think I am police force material.

Since no one was calling me back I was getting desperate. I came up with the idea of becoming a fitness instructor. After I got my certification I started looking for a job but got no results. I decided to try and open my own fitness business but with no capital and my poor social and marketing skills I was unable to get anything off the ground.

I had used up all my unemployment and had no job, or money. I moved into my car, scrounging showers from acquaintances, and having meltdowns over my situation. Then a friend, the woman who had driven me to my interviews while I was in the Safe House, offered me a job as a cook in their home. While I was there they gave me some suggestions for finding regular employment. I thought that looking at the newspaper was too old school and I wouldn't find anything but there was a posting for home health care work. I applied on site and was hired.

The work was difficult and unpleasant. I had trouble getting along with my clients and rarely worked full time. However, because I was working I lost my food stamps. I should have appealed the decision because it was based on me working full time which I was not. But I was way too overwhelmed to do that. I continued looking for other work but kept striking out. Then I started dating A. Soon after that my friend asked me to move out. I think they thought they were doing me a favor by forcing me to get back on my feet, but all it did was force me to move in with A way too soon. Had I not been forced into that situation I would have never stayed with A as long as I did. He lied to me about everything.

Chapter 19
Rebounding Again

The one good thing that came out of my relationship with A was a job in my field. I found a job near him working as a HAZMAT safety officer for a small university. The job seemed very promising and I could see myself retiring from there. During the interview they told me they were looking for someone who could work independently with minimal supervision. I told them that was exactly what I needed, that I did my best with minimal supervision and did not handle lots of supervision well. I was hired.

During my first few days on the job, I felt like someone had placed me in a maze with a blindfold on, and my hands tied behind my back. There was no one to tell me what to do. After a few hours of mulling over my situation I started looking around the office for clues, and found a list of emergency contacts for each department. I started calling to arrange a walkthrough of the labs. I spent the next two weeks going through all the labs taking notes and making suggestions. I told them this was not a lab inspection but if I saw something I felt needed to be addressed quickly I would tell them. By the time I finished the walkthroughs I had an action plan in my head. There was a lot of work to do, but I was on fire to get things done. My predecessor had left almost a year prior, and she had been a grad student. She did her best but fell short on a lot of things. It was a lot for one person to do, let alone a full time grad student, and things had gotten worse since she left.

I ran into my first trouble when there was a mercury release at the student clinic. I was in the middle of teaching a safety training class and told them I would be there when I was done. They did not like that. They wanted me to drop everything and run over and deal with it. All my years dealing with spills had taught me that spills take time. Days, sometimes weeks, to my mind there was no rush, they were adamant. So I let someone else take over my class and went over there. As I suspected they wanted me to go in and quickly clean it up so everyone could get back to their business. It wasn't that simple. I didn't have a spill cleanup kit, someone brought me one, but I still couldn't do it. I had no detection equipment, no way of knowing where the mercury was, and no way of knowing if I had gotten it all. This was a sensitive area where sick and possibly pregnant students would be spending time in. It had to be done right. My predecessor would have let herself get bullied into going in and just swept up what she could see, but I knew that wasn't enough. Mercury breaks up into millions of tiny microscopic balls that go everywhere, and you can't see them. Had this been an ordinary space it would have been different but not a clinic.

State police suggested getting EPA in to clean it up, and campus police wanted to go ahead with that plan. I thought we should try a contractor first. It was Friday afternoon. I was supposed to be leaving for a backpacking trip in a few hours but knew it wasn't happening. So I cancelled it. That was the last time I signed up for a backpacking trip. They were very angry at me for cancelling the last minute, and I knew I would never be able to commit 100% while I was in that position. By the next morning I hadn't found a contractor that could make it within a day or two, and decided to call EPA. It was Saturday so EPA was closed. I called the National Response Center because I knew they were open 24/7/365. They gave me a number but it was EPA's closed offices. I called back, and they told me that was the only number they could give me. I asked them if I could give them my number to give to the EPA on call person. My years of incident response had taught me a few things. The NRC agreed to that and within an hour someone from EPA called me back. We discussed the situation and they told me they would be in town the next day and start work Monday morning.

It took EPA five days working with two sets of contractors to finish that cleanup. Pieces of carpet had to be removed, some equipment was too contaminated and had to be removed. EPA praised my response, the university was still angry about it. They still wanted me to have just gone in and swept up the mess and called it done. I told them things were going to have to change, that the university would have to start doing things the correct way.

I made a lot of changes the first few months and people weren't happy about it but it was the correct way to do things. Despite all the pushback I stood my ground that this was how things had to be done and over time found more and more evidence that years ago, things were done right at the university. But when their last knowledgeable HAZMAT safety officer left over ten years ago things started falling apart. My predecessor had fixed some of it but did not know how to stand up and say, this is not my responsibility, this needs to be handled by lab personnel. Besides the regulations saying it, there was no way one person could do everything safety related in hundreds of labs. They ran my predecessor ragged trying.

Getting faculty to cooperate was my biggest hurdle, and would plague me for the rest of my time there. There were a few who were very cooperative, but the rest completely ignored me. After a few months I found out about forums and conferences for professionals who did safety at universities, and signed up for a training for people who were new to the profession. Despite my experience there were a lot of new things I was dealing with so I signed up. During that training I realized I had to change my approach.

When I know and understand why I need to create change I can do it with enthusiasm. I started changing how I did everything. Some of the tensions eased but getting faculty to cooperate was still a huge problem. I decided to focus on the things I had more control over first, my office, and the 90 day storage. I had not seen either of them before I started the job. My office was full of stuff from the past 50 years. I started thinning things out, getting rid of old books and catalogues, then tackled the filing cabinets that were full of files for faculty members that were no longer at the university.

The 90 day storage was a much bigger task. The first time I walked in there my reaction was, "Oh my god, what have I gotten myself into."

There was so much old waste all over, I wasn't sure where to start. This was something I had never dealt with. I found a contents list the interim had made, she has my gratitude for that, and contacted the waste disposal company the university worked with. I sent them the list and they gave me a date and time they would be there. It was a disaster and I knew I had to find another company. They showed up with one B truck for two days, and sent a crew that couldn't handle unknowns which was one of the things that had been on the list. They took the newest waste and left everything else. The old waste had to go. The university had been holding onto things "in case it might be needed in the future." This is called speculative accumulation, and is a violation. Without even seeing the last inspection from the hazardous waste bureau I knew this had to be done. Later I would find out that it had been written up as a violation and that my predecessor had sent them a letter saying everything had been disposed of.

The next day, like magic, a representative from another company showed up at my door. They presented a very compelling case to hire them, but I knew I couldn't make the decision on my own. I told them I would have to talk to my supervisor first.

My supervisor asked me if I had talked to anyone who had worked with them and I said, "No, that's a really good idea."

They had given me some client names. I heard nothing but good things from their clients so my supervisor agreed to the change. They offered solutions to the more problematic waste streams I had identified, though I would later learn there was so much more, and were also charging a lot less than the previous company. After a walk through the 90 day storage the new company said they would book two weeks to get the building cleared out. During those two weeks we dealt with several explosives, including several pounds of concentrated benzoyl peroxide. They told me they had seen worse storage areas but never anything with the variety we had there. Being a research facility so many chemicals and dangerous materials had been used over the years. There were chemicals from the 1920's 1940's and 1950's. I'm sure there were chemicals from other time periods, but those were the ones that stood out to me. They ended up staying a third week. On the last day they stayed until almost midnight. We had to finish. I was going for my Radiation Safety Officer training the next day. I had agreed to take on more responsibilities in return for a raise. The final manifest was about fifty pages long but we got it all. I had my student worker clean the building while I was in training.

Before she left my predecessor told me that they university had historically been a small quantity generator (SQG) but got bumped up to a large quantity generator during the last inspection by the state and she didn't know why. After I saw the 90 day storage I understood why. An SQG can accumulate up to 1 kg (2.2 lbs.) per month of acutely hazardous waste, which means it can have a maximum of 6 Kg (13.2 lbs.) in storage at any given time. There were hundreds of pounds of acutely hazardous waste in that 90 day storage. For those of you doing the math, an SQG can store waste up to 180 days.

I started offering lab clean outs to faculty to try and get as much waste out of the labs as I could. I wanted to downgrade us back down to an SQG at the beginning of the next year which would mean I would have to be more careful with my waste accumulation. Overall, I removed several tons of hazardous waste from the university and almost half a ton of acutely hazardous waste in my first year.

Next I tackled the radioactive materials storage area. I managed to convince my supervisor that we needed a contractor for this as well. Using the contractor, we were able to decontaminate and classify most of the waste in the storage area as non-radioactive which would end up saving several times more than the cost of the contractor was in waste disposal fees. I didn't have the licensing or detection equipment to do that myself. All I had was a Geiger counter, and that isn't enough to declassify potentially radioactive items.

I learned how to certify the fume hoods myself instead of paying a contractor to come in every year and do them, found us affordable online university focused safety trainings, rewrote all the safety protocols for the university, created guidance documents, and was part of the team rewriting the universities outdated emergency response protocols. Because I was, for the most part, being left alone to figure things out I was highly motivated, and was driving myself hard. I was meeting with my supervisor about once a month, mostly to talk about how I was going to continue bringing the university into compliance, and create a safety culture. Some of my ideas got vetoed, but most were accepted.

While I was dealing with all those things and much more, I was working on revamping lab inspections. I decided to call them safety reviews and make them by appointment rather than surprise inspections. I did all of this to make the faculty more comfortable with the process but they still refused to cooperate and give me dates. I decided I had to start doing surprise inspections after all. Then something called Covid-19 started being talked about in the news. I got a handful of inspections done, and the university shut down. I couldn't even finish certifying the fume hoods that year.

Chapter 20
Covid 19

Six months before the pandemic started I got a new supervisor C. She was working under my previous supervisor and would be overseeing several other programs. I was very upset over the change at first but things went well those first few months. She wasn't trying to micromanage me, and that was all I really cared about. I asked to continue working from my office. I didn't have internet at home and since a few of the labs would still be operating on a smaller capacity I should be on campus in case I was needed. C immediately agreed with my reasoning and I was able to continue my routine of going to the office every day.

Campus was like a ghost town but I liked it that way. I would sometimes go to work on the weekend to work in silence, and now I had it all the time. Every once in a while I would run into another person and it would startle me. The only thing I was upset about was not being able to dance. But it was only for six weeks and I felt I could handle that. I kept saying to myself like a mantra, "it's only six weeks, it's no big deal."

When the lockdowns became permanent for an indeterminate amount of time my anxiety skyrocketed. Every time someone would say "our lives will never be the same," I had a meltdown. This time I knew I was having meltdowns, I was telling other people I was having meltdowns, I just didn't know they were related to autism. I knew the suicidal thoughts couldn't be too far down the road. I tried calling the suicide hotline but because I wasn't actively suicide they got me off the line quickly. I could tell they didn't want to bother with me. Over the last ten years, after Miri died, and I had decided not to get another cat. I was working full time and doing part time grad school. The need to have a social life gripped me. It wasn't just that Miri was gone. My experience with D had shown me that being isolated was not a good thing. If I had more friends there would be more people I could ask for help if things started to go wrong for me. So I had developed a social life, and it was suddenly all gone. Had the pandemic happened before that I would have been fine. Now it was a change I couldn't handle.

It wasn't just loneliness that was driving my meltdowns. Over the ten years I danced I realized that dancing helped me maintain my mental health, and greatly improved my emotional regulation. Whenever I would have to go for more than a few days without dancing I would start to become irritable and anxious. As soon I stepped back on the dance floor I would start to calm down, and two hours of dancing gave me relief for several days. Partner dancing is one of the best therapies for trauma, anxiety, and depression.

The loneliness that gripped me was so soul wrenching, I even considered contacting A. That would have been a disaster. To deter myself I started obsessively watching podcast after podcast on narcissism. Watching those videos I realized this was also my mother, so I started looking for podcasts on narcissistic mothers. All the podcasts I watched were by licensed clinicians. I stayed away from anyone who wasn't a licensed clinician. Then I found a podcast on the effects of narcissistic mothers on their daughters and decided to look up the clinician. On her website she had a document that talked about attachment theory. Light bulbs were going off in my head. I tried to see if I could get some sessions with her through the universities employee mental health program but she wasn't on the approved list. I decided to try someone from the university list but it was a disaster.

The therapist never asked me about my childhood. She just suggested things like go for a walk every day, I was already walking to and from work every day, often twice a day. It was only a quarter mile each way but I didn't see how walking more would make a difference. The last time I became suicidal I was outdoors all the time. She suggested I dance with a pillow in my living room. I thought that was the most ridiculous thing I had ever heard. A big part of what makes partner dancing so magical for me is the connection to another person. This desire to connect through activity rather than chatting is very common with autistics.

There is something about moving around a dance floor in perfect sync with another person that I find exhilarating, and emotionally healing. Solo dancing does nothing for me and I hate it. I found myself watching an ecstatic dance one day. I had heard the music and went to investigate. The person at the door told me to come in, the first time was free but something held me back. I stood there for about fifteen to twenty minutes trying to figure out why I found this so troubling. Eventually it hit me. Dance is a language, and when you dance with other people you are having a conversation about the music and expressing it with your body. Watching all these people dancing alone surrounded by other people was like being in a large room with a lot of people talking out loud without anyone talking to anyone else. It was all very disturbing and I walked away. Unfortunately, because of the state I was in, I was having trouble speaking, and couldn't explain myself to her. The therapist finally told me I was choosing to be depressed, and I wanted nothing more to do with her. I decided to find a way to work with the other therapist even though she was in another state.

Since I couldn't afford to pay for the therapist out of pocket myself I decided to work with someone else in her practice who cost almost half as much. It was still a lot of money but if it would help me deal with my struggles it would be worth it. I knew it wasn't just my parents, that D had played a huge role in whatever was plaguing me, but the therapist I started working with disagreed. He insisted it was all tied to my childhood. In a way he was right, but he was also very wrong. D played a huge part in my developing CPTSD. I have discussed all of this with my current therapist. He wasn't a bad therapist, just trained by his mentor to see everything through a certain lens. He helped me work through some issues I had never opened up to anyone about that plagued me for decades. Things I have not written about because even though I have finally started to heal, writing about them would be too difficult. They were like gaping open wounds in my psyche for decades. I have not healed enough to feel safe enough to pick at the scabs that have formed over those gaping wounds, and they would not add enough to the narrative to be worth the risk. I am very grateful for his help with those things, and for helping me examine and understand the seeds my parents had planted in my brain.

After about ten sessions I realized that the methodology he wanted to teach me wouldn't work for me. He wanted me to learn to recognize I was getting triggered, identify where a trigger was coming from, acknowledge it, remind myself that this was the past, and move on. I knew I couldn't do that, but I didn't know why, and I didn't know how to explain it. I understand it now. I had no control over my emotions, and no way of gaining any control over my emotions without knowing I was autistic, and understanding the overwhelm, meltdown, shutdown cycles I go through. It is possible that over time, once I have healed enough, I might be able to learn how to control my emotions now that I am aware of these things and understand how they impact me. Maybe not completely, but at least partially.

While I was doing those therapy sessions I came across a book called The Body Keeps the Score by Dr. Bessel Van der Kolk. While reading that book I realized I had CPTSD, and discussed it with the therapist, he confirmed it for me. While reading that book I found out that ballroom dancing is a recommended therapy for people with C/PTSD. In the book Dr. Van der Kolk also discusses various treatments he had seen successfully help people with PTSD. I decided to try neurofeedback. Most people choose EMNRD, but I had too many traumas to deal with, and suspected I couldn't remember some of them. Even though it would be expensive Neurofeedback seemed like the better path for me. I found a provider and started the sessions. The results were remarkable. I went from crying nonstop to smiling and laughing in a few short weeks. I felt like I was on cloud nine and that nothing could get to me. I had never been happier in my life. It was like I was in love, but not with a person, just in love with life. My focus was back, I started devouring books again, something I had not been able to do since developing CPTSD. I was running again, was taking initiatives at work again, nothing was going to stop me.

The drive for self-improvement was burning in me, I signed up for group classes with a dating coach. I wanted to figure out what I was doing wrong. Things started out well, I was excelling at this coursework as much as any other training I had ever done, and started to understand some of the toxic things I was doing in relationships like jumping in and trying to solve everyone's problems for them, and using some toxic verbiage during arguments. Then disaster struck.

The dating coach set up mock dating sessions for us to practice what we had learned on each other. The first few went well enough, then a new group came in and joined the mock dating. I got paired with one of them. One of the things we were supposed to do was critique the background and overall presentation of the person. Unfortunately, this person looked like she was sitting in a dungy warehouse and I asked her if she was at work and if there was anywhere else she would be able to "date" from. She took offense and said I was being mean to her. I explained the parameters of the exercise but she refused to listen. When we rejoined the group I knew what was going to happen. When the dating coach called on her she said that someone had been mean to her. I was expecting this. The dating coach immediately went on the defensive and starting apologizing to her for being treating badly. I was not expecting that. The dating coach should have known no one in the group was being mean, instead she went on and on about how terrible it was that someone had been mean to her and so did everyone else. I felt under attack. I was back at the dinner table with my family being ganged up on and put down. Finally with relish the woman named me and the dating coach started backpedaling because she knew there was no way I had been mean but the damage was done. I was in meltdown.

The dating coach called me later to tell me I had done nothing wrong but it was too late. It wasn't just that I had been attacked and humiliated. I didn't like the way she handled the whole situation and didn't want to learn how to behave from someone who had handled the situation so badly. I asked for my money back and she agreed. It was part of the contract that we could ask for our money back at any time throughout the course. I took the whole thing as a sign, came to the conclusion that I was not dating material, and that there was no point in ever trying again. After receiving my autism diagnosis, I felt even more strongly about this. Even though I know that a good relationship would do wonders for me, I recognize now that it will never happen. No mentally healthy man is going to want me. All I can attract is more abuse.

One thing I learned from that whole experience is the importance of communicating through storytelling. During the first lesson the coach read two versions of an introductory message, one was more detailed and descriptive, the other was more terse and to the point. I resonated with the latter but everyone else in the class resonated more with the former. Over the rest of that lesson, and the mock dating sessions she hammered into us the importance of communicating through storytelling. The mock dating sessions were an opportunity for us to share our stories with each other and get feedback on them. This is why I decided to share my story with the world. The best way to get through to people is by sharing your story.

***

My original concept for this book was one of multiple stories from multiple late diagnosed autistics, but I couldn't find anyone else who wanted to share their story. It's not easy to tell the world about your struggles. Eventually I had to accept that this would be a solo venture, but I hope others will start sharing their stories too so the rest of the world can see how diverse the autistic community is, while recognizing that our struggles are real. Coming from one person, it might seem that I am exaggerating or looking for excuses. Nothing could be further from the truth. Each struggle has been extremely difficult to write about because of the feelings of shame associated with them. But owning them is part of accepting them, and learning from them. You can't grow without healing, and you can't heal without processing, and you can't process without accepting, and you can't accept without knowing what to accept. This has been my lifelong block, not knowing what to accept because I didn't know who I was.

Another reason I had for wanting multiple autistic people in this narrative is that there are many things other autistics struggle with that I don't, and things I struggle with that others don't. Only about one third of autistics have situational mutism. Some are nonverbal, and many nonverbal autistics are highly intelligent, we don't know why they can't speak. Each autistic has their own unique set of challenges which is why it is a spectrum. The spectrum isn't linear, it's a sphere. Many autistics who have a completely different set of talents and abilities from mine deal with some of the things I deal with. This was the rationale for creating the spectrum in 2013. In some ways it has united the autistic community, but it has also harmed high masking autistics who are now considered no different from someone like "Rainman." I choose to call myself autistic rather than someone with Aspergers because we need to fight the stigmas associated with autism rather than splinter off and say "we are not like them," because we are like them in many ways.

Besides having different comorbidities, and struggles, how we experience similar issues can differ from autistic to autistic. I am sure there are some autistics who don't struggle at all with showering, though I haven't met one yet. But we each have a different struggle. One can't stand the feeling of their wet hair on their skin, another can only shower after a workout because they need to feel sweaty and uncomfortable to be able to get into the shower, I can't stand the sensation of toweling off. We are each of us so unique.

***

Before the mock dating incident happened I had already decided on my next project, so I signed for a course to learn how to meditate. The closest I had ever gotten to being able to meditate was while I was counting strides running, and on the dance floor. In order to follow I had to completely let go and stop thinking, it was a form of meditation. But I was determined to be able to master real meditation now and through perseverance was having some success. At first I could only meditate it for a few minutes at a time, but I was eventually able to stay in it for twenty to thirty minutes. I was feeling the positive effects, and it was helping me deal with all the negativity I was running into.

Soon after the pandemic shut downs started my supervisor had started to change. She suddenly became very autocratic and demanding. After finishing my neurofeedback trainings, I was working on two presentations, one internal for faculty, and one for a conference. They were both within a few days and I was feeling the pressure because one of them was about some software I had not used in years and I was having trouble remembering all the ins and outs of how to make it work. This was for the conference. My supervisor decided to demand I put something together that I had no idea how to approach at that moment. I told her I would do it next week after the conference presentation. She insisted I do it within two days. She had never been demanding like that before. I had a meltdown, and she got angry with me. The conference presentation did not go well. Things of this nature continued to happen. It felt as if she couldn't stand that I had fixed myself and was determined to tear me down.

Switching tasks can be very difficult for autistics. Most of the time I handle it very well, but, occasionally I struggle with it because my brain feels like it's stuck in thick mud. Because I was dealing with a deadline that I was struggling with I was already anxious, frustrated, and overwhelmed. Under those circumstances I couldn't handle the task change. Some things I could handle, like an incident in a lab, because I knew they were part of my job, and had a built in understanding that this could interrupt my day. Things that were not built into my mind as reasonable interferences create blocks in my brain that feel like it's being dragged through thick mud. It can take me anywhere from a few minutes to a few days to recover depending on the level of overwhelm it generates. There was no rush with what she was requesting, it could have easily waited for a few days. Her anger seemed to be over her inability to control me. That was never going to happen, I have never been controllable in that way by other people, and never will be. I had told the university I didn't handle tight supervision well and they had hired me knowing this.

Another memorable incident was when the VP for research decided I needed to take over some responsibilities regarding items belonging to a section of the university I had minimal dealings with. They were a large research center and had their own safety staff. When I asked for more information C said she would try and get it for me but never did. A few months later she told me she had signed me up for a training related to these items and I had a meltdown because I didn't know what they were. I starting sending emails to everyone I could think of demanding to know what it was, and C was furious at me for my unprofessional behavior. I tried to explain to her that I needed more information but she wasn't listening to me. She demanded that I control myself, and I knew I couldn't, I just couldn't explain why. All I knew was that I had CPTSD, and that it was probably triggered, and that wasn't enough for her. She demanded I control myself better in the future, but I didn't know how I would be able to do this. I told her that in order to behave better I needed my questions answered, and that made her angrier.

Before getting my CPTSD diagnosis I was completely in the dark about what I was struggling with. The CPTSD diagnosis shined a light on things. But I didn't realize at the time that it was just a candle, and all my attempts to understand my erratic emotions and behavior were hindered because at no time could I see the entire picture. Most of it was still in the shadows. When I got the ASD diagnosis it was as if the main light switch had been flipped and I could suddenly see and examine everything going on in my mind, and start understanding what was driving me during my struggles.

Whenever I reminded the university that I was hired to a position that required someone who could work independently with minimal supervision I would be told that things change and that I needed to adjust. I was not able to adjust. Despite the neurofeedback I was still autistic, and though the CPTSD symptoms had subsided they were not completely eradicated. But I kept asking for what I needed in a desperate attempt to get them to understand. The problem was, I didn't really understand it myself, so I couldn't properly explain it to them. Still, denying my needs was tantamount to refusing to give a person in a wheelchair access to a ramp or elevator, and demanding that they adjust to going up the stairs. No one would do that to someone in a wheelchair, but with an invisible disability it's easy to dismiss the persons needs because you can't see them, and if you can't see them you can't conceptualize them which leads people to dismissing them as "they are just looking for an excuse, and they just need to try harder." But invisible disabilities are just as real as those you can see.

Things weren't too bad for the next six months. Despite some clashes with my supervisor, and the never ending catch up meetings she was scheduling, the neurofeedback training along with the meditations were keeping me in equilibrium, and other than a few meltdowns during these clashes, and the difficulty dealing with all the unnecessary meetings, I was feeling good about myself, was happy, and productive. The catch up meetings were affecting me more than I realized. Every autistic I have heard talking about work difficulties has described how difficult meetings are for them. Meaningful meetings about something substantial have never been a problem for me. I understand that they are an important part of the process of getting things done when multiple people are involved. But the catch up meetings made no sense to me and were pure torture. I did my best, but they were like idle chit chat, and I cannot handle idle chit chat for more than a few minutes. Those meetings were absolute nightmares for me. But it would take me months to be able to express my discomfort over them because I was doing my best to suppress my discomfort, and by then a lot of damage was done. The constant interruptions and mind blocks they created in me were affecting my ability to focus. They also became triggering because I kept asking to not have my office moved in them and was constantly denied that need.

Then I had to deal with a piece of equipment in one of the labs that had a lot of mercury in it, and it was structurally unsound. I brought in our transporter and we dismantled it and got it out of the lab for disposal, but some mercury spilled and we cleaned it up. There were a few more releases that had to be dealt with before it was fully packed away and ready for transport. I went home as soon as we were done, removed my clothes at the doorway, put them in a trash bag outside the door, showered, then put the bag in the trash. Then I drove to the hospital to check for mercury exposure. I had done things on the fly without proper planning and was worried about exposure. The hospital insisted there was no need to test me because the mercury wasn't vaporized I couldn't have a high enough exposure. I was angry they wouldn't listen to me but looking back, I don't think it would have made a difference. The test would have come back negative even though I know I had some exposure. At that moment I decided to let it go.

Two days later I left work early so I could go camping with a Meetup group I had not interacted with before. I was excited to get out and do something with other people. Other than some online Meetups, my social life was still dead and I was anxious to get back to it. Since camping was an outdoor activity it seemed safe enough. But I was feeling sluggish and was worried about the three hour drive, so I decided to go for a quick run to perk myself up. About two minutes after I started jogging my foot hit a rock. This happened almost every time I went for a run, often multiple times during a run, because I ran on dirt roads, and it had never been an issue. That day I lost my balance and fell. My right arm instinctively went out to break my fall, and I felt a sharp pain in my right shoulder. I laid there for about ten minutes unable to move, and unsure of how long I would have to wait for someone to come by and help me. After ten minutes I managed to pull myself up and slowly sluggishly made my way back home. I tried moving my arm and it didn't seem that bad, but over the next hour it got progressively worse until I couldn't move it at all. I cancelled my trip and contacted a clinic, they told me to go to the ER. I managed to get my car into gear with my left hand and slowly made my way to the hospital. They admitted me and eventually a doctor came by and asked about my pain level. I am not good at gauging my pain level, I said 8, I should have said 10. He started to manipulate my arm and I had a delayed reaction with my pain. I had trained myself over the years to suppress things, I had to remind myself to react to the pain and not suppress. The doctor said he didn't think there was any skeletal damage but he would do an x-ray to be sure. I could tell he had already made up his mind, and he came back saying the x-rays were clean. I still couldn't move my arm.

The nurse helped me put my shirt back on and they gave me a sling. I could tell the nurse thought I was overreacting with my pain. She suggested some movement exercises to prevent my shoulder from freezing up, but the pain when I tried them, was unbearable.

There is no way to prove it, but I know that I lost my balance because of the mercury exposure. I have a hyper sensitivity to chemicals, and combined with my vestibular sensory issues it wouldn't take much for my balance to be affected. I didn't know about my vestibular sensory issues at the time, or have any way of conveying any of this at the time.

The fall occurred on a Friday, I stayed home until Wednesday. On Thursday I had appointments to certify fume hoods in a building that had just been renovated and faculty was eager to move into the labs and start working. With my arm in the sling and my student worker doing most of the work I made my way through the labs testing the fume hoods. My supervisor had to tie my shoes for me that day, I had no dexterity in my right hand. After a few hours I had to stop, the pain was too much. The next day I went back and finished the fume hoods.

For the next few weeks, I continued to work partial days. All my plans for the summer had to be scrapped, both personally and for work. I did the essentials and nothing more, I was in too much pain, and was having trouble sleeping because of the pain. What I didn't realize was the amount of sensory overwhelm I was in. All I knew was that my head would start spinning, nausea was kicking in, and exposure to light became too painful after a few hours. It was all because of my shoulder pain as I thought, but it was creating severe autistic overwhelm that I couldn't recognize.

The one essential thing I couldn't do was drive my work truck. It was an old manual gear Chevy pickup, and some of the gears would stick. I didn't have the range of motion or the strength in my right arm to move the gears and there was no way to do it with my left arm. This meant I couldn't do waste pickups. I tried teaching my student worker to drive manual gear but, the truck with its finicky clutch was a terrible vehicle to learn on, and it didn't go well. After a few weeks the pain had subsided enough and I had enough range of motion to try, so I set up waste pickups. My student worker would have to do all the lifting but at least I could get us around campus. I think I would have been OK if there hadn't been a blocked road that forced me to drive all the way around campus to get to the last building. I was starting to feel my shoulder again.

As we drove back the pain got worse and worse. I told C I wouldn't be able to do this for a while. She felt this was a core duty and decided

161

to consult with human resources. Human resources told her that I had to be sent home because my job description said 70% heavy lifting and I clearly couldn't lift. I pointed out to C that it also said 70% sitting, there was clearly a mistake there.

She responded with, "That's what we have to work with so you have to go home until we get clearance from a doctor for you to lift."

At that point I was in so much pain that I was fine going to a doctor and figuring out what was going on, and even taking some time off, but there was so much that needed to be done, and I could still do the majority of my work. C insisted that we had to do what HR was saying there was no way around it. There was in fact some heavy lifting associated with my position but it was incidental rather than a mainstay of my job. I could count on one hand the number of times I had done heavy lifting (over 50 lbs.) in the last three years.

The earliest doctor's appointment I was able to get was three weeks out. During that time C called me constantly but I didn't answer my phone, she came to my house and I didn't answer the door. She had sent me home, I wasn't going to respond. My therapist says I had the right to set that boundary. If I was off the clock I was off the clock. What I didn't understand was that I didn't want to talk to anyone because I was in shutdown from the pain, and heading for an autistic burnout from the constant overwhelm. I had months of leave saved up so I wasn't worried in that regard, but sitting at home with nothing but my pain to deal with was wreaking havoc on my mental health, and I couldn't meditate. I wasn't taking any pain medication. I had finally fixed my constipation issues and wasn't going to mess it up again with pharmaceuticals. I was used to suppressing and did my best to suppress the pain but it was too overwhelming, making it impossible to meditate.

The orthopedic surgeon set up an appointment for an MRI. The earliest available date was over two weeks out, and by the time the day came around the pain had almost completely gone away. I almost called to cancel the MRI but decided not to, and it was a good thing I didn't cancel. The MRI found a fracture on my humerus and a partially torn tendon. I got a referral letter for physical therapy, and set it up as soon as I got back to town. The orthopedic surgeon was about 90 miles away, I needed something local. The next day I went to work but got sent home after a few hours. HR still wanted me to be able to do heavy lifting before I was allowed back. I was fuming. I started an email argument back and forth with my supervisor copying HR on it saying my job description was wrong and I had plenty to do that had no heavy lifting, or any lifting at all. Eventually everyone suddenly relented and said my job description could be changed, but that I would have to stay home until it was officially done.

My previous supervisor, who was my current supervisor's supervisor, set up a meeting between the three of us. Even though I was still on leave I decided to go in order to clear the air between us. The meeting did not go very well. I was told to get therapy for my CPTSD and learn to deal with things better, I would not be able to get any accommodations. They would not give me my old office back. I was told that I was now part of a group and had to be in the same building with the group. I pointed out that there was no connection between what we did, that I didn't understand what anyone else did, and they didn't understand what I did, and that I couldn't handle the changes. I was told that change happens and I had to adjust. I reminded them that I had been told the job required someone who could work independently with minimal supervision, and got the same response, "You need to adjust."

I couldn't adjust. Any ability I had to adjust to change had been subsumed by the overwhelm of my pain, and the injustice of being sent home for months for no reason. During that meeting my previous supervisor pointed out that I had communication issues before C became my supervisor. He said that I had given him some tips on how to communicate with me to prevent my overreaction. I told him I had asked C to change how she communicated with me but she had refused. Now she suddenly agreed, though reluctantly. Unfortunately, it never happened. Her communications became more and more demanding, more and more triggering, more and more unbearable.

Chapter 21
Back at Work

I t took a few more days for me to be able to return to work. I started going through my emails and my calendar, and saw a presentation scheduled for Friday morning that I had completely forgotten about. That presentation became my priority because I didn't have a topic for it, and would have to figure out what I wanted to talk about and then put the power point and materials together. Stress and overwhelm gripped me but I forced myself to start thinking about it.

C barged into my office seething about a credit card report I had not handed in. I told her I had other more pressing things to deal with and would take care of it the following week but she insisted I had to get it done by the end of the next day. My stress levels were so high at that point that my brain felt like it was being dragged through thick mud trying to incorporate this new task into my day along with the presentation. I saw no other option. I contacted the chemistry department and cancelled the presentation. When C found out I had cancelled a presentation she got even angrier at me. She said she expected me to tell her that I had other commitments that needed to be attended to, except that I had done that. Visions of my mother calling me worthless started popping up.

There were in fact multiple credit card reports I had not handed in. When the pandemic started I didn't know what to do about them and there was no guidance coming out, at least, none that I was receiving. I contacted the woman who reviewed them for me to ask how to get them to her because I had a problem with my scanner. Up until that point I had been going to the main research office to use their scanner but it was now locked all the time and I didn't have keys because it was in another building. She replied back that email would be great, and I was too overwhelmed to pursue it any more. I made a few attempts to put together the report but couldn't get it done. The stress of the pandemic shutdowns was so overwhelming that I quickly went into overload and couldn't function. This loss of executive functions

164

is a clear sign that I was in autistic burnout, but of course, I had no clue at the time. I decided to stop trying until someone contacted me about them so I could get better guidance but no one ever did, so I decided I would do them when we got out of lockdown. When we got out of lockdown I was on forced leave. It was now a huge issue and C was very angry with me. She insisted that guidance had gone out but I never saw any. I know I messed up but so did a lot of other people. In the past I was once a few days late with a report because I was waiting for a receipt I knew was in the mail. Within a day I was contacted about it. Now, for over a year, no one had contacted me. If I had misused the card I would have understood C's anger, but I never did that. I don't think I am capable of doing something like that. That would be stealing and I get upset if I accidentally walk away with someone's pen.

It is hard to say with confidence when I went from merely being in a bad shutdown to autistic burnout, but, I think the day I had to cancel the presentation to do the credit card reports may have been the catalyst. I was physically ill by the time I finished those reports and had to go home or I was going to vomit. I was so dizzy and nauseated I couldn't function the rest of the day, and dealing with change was getting harder and harder.

Next C handed me FMLA paperwork to fill out so I could get the time off to do my physical therapy. I refused to fill out the paperwork, and she got even angrier with me. I was too overwhelmed to handle anything new like that and decided to stop going to physical therapy rather than do the paperwork. My overwhelm was through the roof. Not only was I still dealing with the pain from my shoulder, and the difficulty of dealing with the changed location, but I had to deal with all the sensory issues from my new office. My desk had been placed right behind the window and there was too much light. It was bolted down and could not be moved. The building was much noisier, and I could hear every move the woman in the office next to mine made. I yearned for the dark quiet sanctuary of my previous office.

C started looking for reasons to attack me. I had not been able to set up the voicemail on my university cell phone. She suggested I have my student worker do it and I thought that was a good idea. My student worker spent about half an hour working on the phone then handed it to me saying it was working, except it wasn't. I believe he set it up, there was something wrong with the phone. C started insisting that I get the voicemail set up on my phone, I kept telling her there was something wrong with the phone and she said I should go to the company and get it fixed but I was already so deep into autistic burnout that I was losing executive function. Things that were usually easy for me to do became extremely difficult, some became impossible. There was no way I could handle a new task, and no way to explain myself.

At least once a week C would find a reason to yell at me. Every time she came into my office I saw my mother towering over me and yelling at me. I would barely recover from one episode and another one would start. Most of the time I was too shut down to function, and every time I started to recover I got attacked again. Throughout all of this I was under the impression that I was only dealing with CPTSD triggers, I knew nothing about autistic overwhelm, meltdown, and shutdown. My sleep was getting worse, and I was starting to miss appointments with faculty because I couldn't remember anything. The more C attacked me the worse I got, and the more I messed up, the more reasons she had to yell at me.

C started deliberately sabotaging me. I figured this out when she told me that a faculty member had tried to reach me on my cell phone and couldn't. I asked her how the faculty member had gotten my cell phone number because I wasn't giving it out. C said she had given it to the faculty member. I asked why she did that rather than give my email which was the way I always asked people to contact me. I have already mentioned that I liked to have things in writing so I could review them to make sure I was responding in full, and C knew this. C smirked ever so briefly and said nothing.

During one of our altercations, I finally let out, "Do I need to kill myself to get through to you?"

C said nothing and walked out. I had been having suicidal thoughts for weeks and they were becoming more frequent. I wasn't at the planning stage yet but it wasn't that far off. My loss of executive function was by far the worst it had ever been. That evening C texted me that she was concerned about what I had said and that I should get help and put the suicide prevention hotline number. I had no desire to talk to them, I kept remembering how dismissive they had been the last time I called them. I texted back that if she was really concerned for my wellbeing she would give me the reasonable accommodations I was asking for. C never responded back.

Despite all of this I fought my symptoms and managed to start doing lab safety reviews. I had figured out how to get the faculty to respond while I was at home dealing with my shoulder injury. I spoke with the deans because I would need their cooperation and they supported me so I started implementing my method and it was working. I had two to three reviews scheduled per day, and to get away from C I started taking files home with me so I could just go to main campus and home without having to go into my office. This way I could keep my head clear and focus on my work. This made C even angrier.

C sent me the paperwork for my annual review but between my shoulder injury, the constant triggering, and subsequent lack of sleep, I was suffering from severe memory issues and couldn't think of what I had done that last year so I sent her nothing. This memory loss was very disconcerting because like many high masking autistics, I normally have an excellent memory. When I came in for the review C had written me up and had a compliance letter for me to sign. The compliance letter was full of more changes she wanted to force on me. The more I needed space, the more she pressured me, and forced change on me. The more I repeated what I needed, the more I was told that was my problem and I had to adjust. I wrote to HR, and my former supervisor, and his supervisor asking for the accommodations but no one replied.

In the past, whenever things would get bad I would run away, and start fresh. This time I couldn't run. The thought of finding another job and having to move again exhausted me. I didn't have it in me to run anymore. Then I remembered a lecture I had gone to on disability rights. I had gone to the lecture before getting my CPTSD diagnosis anticipating that at some point a student or faculty member would need accommodations for a lab scenario. I had communicated with the woman via email afterwards so I had her in my email. I decided to ask her for advice. She said I was in a tough situation because I had already been written up, but that the accommodations I was asking for, a return to my original working conditions, seemed reasonable, and that not being able to function without the accommodations I needed could be an excuse for not performing.

Somehow, everyone was ignoring the fact that I was still doing my job, at least, I was doing what I could. I just wasn't willing to do the unnecessary things my supervisor was trying to impose on me out of what seemed to me as sheer spite. C was focusing on unnecessary minutia because she felt the need to control me, and there was nothing she could critique about my actual work. C had no STEM background, she was a JD with an undergrad in women's studies. C had no technical knowledge, and whenever she tried to make a technical comment she got things wrong. When I needed guidance I would turn to my counterparts at other universities through the forums, or contact a state regulator. Because I had been a state regulator I had a much easier relationship with them than my counterparts did. What C was doing was not trying to get me to do my job, she was getting in the way of my ability to function. While I was working under my original working conditions I was able to do my job, now I couldn't. All I needed was the conditions I had before so I could do my job again. No one was listening to me. The disability rights woman gave me some language to use, and agencies I could log a complaint in. I decided to go to the EEOC because it was at the top of the list, but, it turned out to be a bad choice. It would take months before they would even talk to me and I didn't have months.

Using the language I had received, I managed to get a meeting with HR to discuss accommodations. One of the things C had demanded that I do was set up sessions with a therapist from the university's mental health program. I decided to do that because I knew I would be able to get a diagnosis letter that way, and I would need one. I was more informed about therapists now so I kept going to look at their bio when they suggested someone to me and would call back saying no, they don't have the experience. They finally told me to go to the website and pick someone. I found a family therapist that seemed to have the right education and experience. During the sessions whenever I described what was happening at work, the therapist would say, "Oh, I need to talk to her, this is not good," but it never happened.

The therapist provided a letter confirming my CPTSD and Major Depressive Disorder diagnosis along with a list of recommended accommodations. We discussed how things should go. I was worried because I knew I was hanging on by a thread but she was confident I would be able to get what I was asking for. That didn't happen. I was put down and told that what I was asking for was ridiculous and out of the question. It didn't help that I was so dysregulated that I could barely speak. They offered me one tiny accommodation that would not in any way address my needs. I tried to bring up the need for a change in communication style but C said that no one else had a problem with her communications so she clearly wasn't the problem, everyone else agreed with her, and it got shut down. After that I shut down, and was unable to stand up for myself.

The accommodation they offered me was the equivalent of offering someone wheelchair bound crutches after being moved from the first floor to third floor in a building with no ramps or elevators, and expecting them to be able to navigate the stairs, and the rest of the working day with nothing but crutches to get around with, while having those crutches kicked out from underneath them several times a day, and still be able to do their job at the same level they did before.

I left the meeting knowing I had no path forward. All I could envision was ending up on the street again, and this time I knew I didn't have it in me to survive. I was too broken, and I would starve to death, or die of exposure. It was better to die now. My only other option was to get on disability but I wasn't able to get accommodations, what were the chances I could get disability? I wasn't feeling hopeful about it but I emailed HR and demanded to be put on disability. I had been paying into long term disability for four years and I needed it now. Each email became more desperate saying I would kill myself if I couldn't get on disability. I ordered a no antidote rat poison online, and started planning my suicide in detail. I forgot about getting on disability, no one would listen to me anyways, and focused on planning my suicide. This time I would make sure I ate enough to kill me. I would mix it in with food, and force myself to eat all of it. The more I thought about it the more I wanted to die, and the more detailed my plan became, the more I was looking forward to it. Dying would make it all go away. No more judgement, no more put downs, no more misunderstandings, no more failure, no more telling me I'm not trying hard enough, no more telling me there's nothing wrong when I'm in pain, no more loneliness. This would put an end to all my misery. I stopped eating and drinking thinking that I was going to die anyways so what was the point.

One of the reasons people sometimes back down from suicide is by thinking of loved ones. No one had contacted me in over a year to ask how I was. This was partly my fault. When I go into crisis I push people away. While I was dealing with my shoulder injury I drove everyone away from me because I couldn't handle any interactions.

Allistics do this as well, but they usually have at least one person in their life who sticks around through everything, I had no one. No one cared, no one would miss me. I was a failure at everything, there was no one to live for, no one would even know I was gone. This added to my feelings of worthlessness, and drove my desire to die even more.

The therapist had set up safety plan with me, but I didn't want the safety plan. I wanted to die.

Sometime the day after my meeting with HR the police showed up at my door and took me to the local ER. The university must have been worried about liability and called 911. I know it wasn't out of concern for my wellbeing. Months later I saw C from afar walking her dog, and she sneered at me.

When we got to the ER I was asked questions but refused to answer. They wanted me to put on a hospital gown and I refused. They wanted me to sign paperwork and I refused. They asked me if I wanted anything to eat or drink and I refused. All I wanted was to go home, get my poison in the mail and die. I also knew that if I cooperated I would be sent to a psych ward and I didn't want to go there. The doctor who said I had no skeletal damage came in at one point to try and talk to me. I had an opportunity to say what I wanted to say for the past year. "You're the idiot who said I didn't have a fracture."

He walked out and never came back.

After almost two days they brought in a computer and told me the psychiatrist would be speaking to me. The psychiatrist told me that they had been waiting for me to sign the paperwork and put on the hospital gown, but they couldn't wait any longer. The light from the bulbs at the hospital had been hurting my eyes and I complained about it to the psychiatrist, she asked me some questions about it but all I could say was, "I don't know."

I insisted I had the right to die but she talked me down promising me they could help me learn better coping skills. At the time, not understanding autistic burnout and loss of skills, learning better skills sounded like what I needed. In reality I had most of the skills, I just lost them when I went into autistic burnout, or a lesser form of autistic regression. Because I'm autistic all my skills are transient. The psychiatrist promised me that I would have a private room in the psych ward, and that there was a place I could go that specialized in helping people with C/PTSD after the psych ward. She also said that if I don't

170

start cooperating I would be forced. I knew what that meant and knew I didn't have a choice, so under that coercion I signed the paperwork and put on a hospital gown, but I refused the anti-anxiety medication, and the psychiatrist said I was making bad choices. Maybe she was right, but, how could I make good choices not knowing I was autistic, and everything that came along with that fact.

They had to fly me to the city where the hospital with the psych ward was. I was nauseated the entire flight because of the turbulence, and in subsequent ambulance ride the smells from the diesel exhaust were overpowering. When we got there I told the admitting nurse that I had decided to cooperate for now but that if they couldn't help me I was still planning to kill myself. We were allowed to wear street clothes but since I only had the clothes I was wearing I had to alternate between my clothes and the hospital gowns while they were being washed. The hospital socks had a nasty texture but I had to wear them, I had no shoes and we weren't allowed to be barefoot.

After talking to the nurse, I was able to get some water, then after about an hour they had some food for me, but after a few mouthfuls I tasted dairy and left the rest. They insisted there was no cheese but I later saw the menu and there was some cheese in the dish. I hadn't eaten or had anything to drink for almost three days. It would take another 24 hours for me to be able to order meals off the hospital menu and for the rest of the next day I mostly drank water because the meals they brought me were inedible. I would pick off one thing like a piece of fruit, and put the rest back. They had snacks but I couldn't eat them. After a day we started getting little cups with raw vegetables with the snacks and I ate those. The menu didn't have much I could eat, but it was better than the first meals they gave me.

The psychiatrist at the hospital wanted to put me on antidepressants and I refused. Thankfully they weren't going to force me, but the psychiatrist said that if I wasn't going to take any medication maybe I should go home. I said I would think about it but later told her I would stay because if I went home I would definitely just kill myself. The promise of a place I could get real help was something I wanted to give a chance. Every day she suggested I go home, and I wondered why she wanted me to die. On the weekend I saw a different psychiatrist, he seemed much more competent, and I told him that the other psychiatrist wanted me to die because she kept telling me to go home after I told her I would kill myself if I did that. He said he had

171

never heard of psychiatrist wanting their patient to die but on Monday I saw a different psychiatrist. Everyone else saw the psychiatrist who kept telling me to go home.

Most of the time I sat in a side room away from the others because it was too noisy in the main room, and there was no comfortable place to sit in my room. When that room was closed off I would feel displaced. There was one guy who kept hitting on me and I finally started screaming at him to leave me alone. Another guy who was very impaired was following me around like a puppy dog. The other girls did their best to surround me and not let him get too close but I was still freaking out. Even though he was very impaired he was still capable of raping me. When I spoke with the weekend psychiatrist he wandered into the room and I complained to the psychiatrist about him following me around.

"He is mentally ill," the psychiatrist said.

I wanted to say that some of us had been raped, but couldn't get it out.

When I got discharged I was expecting them to have set up for me to go to the place for people with C/PTSD. They provided me with contact information and nothing else. They claimed they were full and were unable to get me in. The only thing they set up for me was a follow up with the therapist I had been seeing. I was relieved to be getting out by then, the private room never happened and I wanted to be alone, and get away from all those scary men. I gave my number to a few of the girls but never heard from any of them.

The poison was waiting for me when I got home, but I was still hoping the place for people with C/PTSD would be able to help me so I put it away, in case I wanted it later. I called the C/PTSD place and found out they had plenty of room. I arranged to go there in two days, I wanted some time to deal with a few things before I left for a month. For about 18 months after becoming suicidal there were still days, moments, when everything is so overwhelming, that I wish I had simply taken the poison and ended my life. But at the time, the promise of a place with other people like me was too tempting. I thought I would finally be in a place where I fit in.

Chapter 22
Residential Care

The C/PTSD place was not what I was expecting. It was mainly a rehab for people with substance abuse issues. Since I had no substance abuse issues I immediately felt out of place. While I was there I had my first known encounter with a transgender woman, and pronouns. Even though I had been working at a university for four years I never had to deal with pronouns because I almost exclusively dealt with faculty and it was a technical university. STEM faculty don't get into social justice issues. There was a small humanities department but I never had any reason to interact with them. All the students I did interact with were STEM majors and none of them ever brought up pronouns. There was an LGBTQ club for the students but I never had anything to do with it. I had always supported equal rights in principle, but it was never anything I had gotten involved in. There were never any visible signs of activism of any kind on campus. Students were way too busy getting their homework done to get involved in that.

The pronouns were incredibly confusing to me. It wasn't just having to had adjust to some people wanting to be called they them to their face which was grammatically incorrect, I had to remember to call people she when they looked like a he, and people were getting angry at me for getting confused and using the wrong pronouns. When I said it was confusing, they stated, "No it's not."

I started to withdraw and isolate as much as I could.

The first cabin I was put in had a transgender woman in it. She had not started her transition yet, and she looked walked, talked and acted like a man. I did my best to stay calm but when she walked in on me in the bathroom while I was on the toilet, there were no locks on any of the doors for safety reasons, I had a gut reaction of alarm. I didn't say anything, or scream (I never scream), but my terror must have been evident on my face. To be honest I would have been troubled by being walked in on by anyone, but this person must have taken it as a personal offense because a few hours later I was told I had to move because I had upset her. The bathroom incident was the only interaction I had with her so it had to be that.

They put me in a cabin right next to the main office. It was noisy with all the foot traffic, and I could hear them through the walls even though there was a device in the cabin that was meant to drown it out. The heat didn't work, the blinds were broken, and I couldn't adjust the shower head. But I was alone in there so I said nothing. Being alone was sheer bliss.

Everyone was gushing about how good the food was, and I was struggling to find something to eat. The night they ordered pizza I had a meltdown. Everything had cheese in it, even the salad. They told me there were leftovers in the refrigerator but I couldn't eat that food when it was fresh, how could I even consider eating it now, and if they could go out and order food for everyone else, why couldn't they get food for me? I went to my room and cried over being ignored and left out yet again. After not eating for two days, I went to scrounge for some food but didn't find much. I decided to only go to the kitchen once a day so I wouldn't constantly feel disappointed. Doing this I changed the dynamic from looking for something to eat, not finding anything, and feeling let down, to choosing to not eat. This created a sense of being in control for me. I had so little control over my life at that time that I needed that sense of control. Eventually I got to see the nutritionist and she backed me up but hardly anything changed.

The first thing I said to the therapist I was assigned to was that I don't belong in this world. I had been feeling like this my whole life, and the world kept confirming it for me. The therapist said I was wrong, and that was the last kind thing he said to me. He constantly seemed to be angry with me, and the group therapy was uncomfortable. At the beginning of each session, we were asked how we felt and to give a color that either represented how we were feeling or something else about us for that day. I kept saying I don't know to these things because I couldn't come up with an answer. I switched groups but never found a group I felt really comfortable with. There was one woman who had been diagnosed with borderline personality disorder, and knowing what I know now I constantly wonder if she isn't autistic.

In the past I would always look at my failures as learning opportunities, as something I could use to grow as a person. Now I was way too broken, and defeated. During one of the art therapy sessions, we were asked to draw a depiction of what failure felt like and then describe what steps we could take to turn things around. I drew a picture of a person falling off a cliff and wrote, "climb the mountain, get pushed off the cliff, recover, climb back up, get pushed down again." The therapist asked me to give some details on how I could rebuild my life and I started screaming at her, "No, no more. I am not climbing that mountain anymore," and ran out crying.

After I got my autism diagnosis I had my first actual EMNRD session. During that session I found myself in a cave with my ancestors who told me it wasn't time for me to die yet, that there was something I still had to do. As we went through each step I balked at the answers my brain was giving me. The therapist would pose a question, turn on the flashing lights, and an answer would pop into my head. The answers came very quickly and I kept searching for another answer but nothing else came up. After giving the whole thing some thought I decided to give in to the answers I was given, and was finally able to give up actively being suicidal. Next I started trying to figure out what I needed to do. A few ideas popped into my head, including the idea of a book to help other undiagnosed autistics recognize their autism popped into my head. The idea of the book stayed with me. It would take me a year to be able to start writing it because I was sure no one would want to hear my failure driven boring story.

My therapist became even more caustic with me after my autism diagnosis and I felt under attack. I wanted to go home and find a therapist who could help me understand the autism. The therapist told me I needed to deal with the PTSD first. He also told me that if I left without his recommendation I would end up having to pay for my stay out of pocket. There was no way I could afford to pay that kind of money, and he knew it. He was manipulating me. But, after refusing to cooperate in the therapy sessions he finally told me who to go to in order to get released early.

The man who was in charge of financials was on my side, he said no one should be forced to stay there if it wasn't going to help them. He was working on his certification to become a therapist and told me he thought autistics were amazing, that we were humanity 2.0 because we were so smart and innovative. This was the first time I heard anything positive about autism since my diagnosis and I latched onto it. I was already starting to deteriorate from not being listened to, but talking to him gave me hope. It took a few more days, and I had to set up my aftercare on my own because the woman who normally set it up was away and my therapist refused to help. I wasn't able to set up anything concrete but left messages with my therapist to set up an appointment the following week and they agreed to let me go home, it was 5 days earlier than my original release date.

As I was driving home there was a message from my therapist saying she was full and that I should get another therapist from the company she was working for. I had seen the other therapists' bios and knew there was no one else I could work with there. I spent the next few days having meltdowns over being rejected by my therapist and looking for a new therapist.

Alone at home I didn't find the solace I was hoping for. I went to talk to a neighbor I had socialized with a few times during the pandemic but my autism diagnosis scared her and she made it clear I was not welcome anymore. That rejection along with my therapist's rejection pushed me deeper into autistic burnout. I collapsed into a puddle and couldn't stop crying.

Eventually I was able to find a therapist who specialized in C/PTSD who was able to see me. He was a kind soul, and tried to be as supportive as he could. He suggested a type of music therapy to help with my insomnia, making the comment that it might not work for me because I hear and see things different. I had heard that we perceive things differently, and started walking around trying to figure out what I was seeing and hearing different from other people. Do trees look different to me? Clouds? Houses? I still don't know.

After a few weeks the therapist went on vacation. At first he texted me every week, then disappeared for over a month, and I felt abandoned and rejected. I was still talking to the social worker he had put me in contact with and she was concerned that I wasn't getting any therapy for such a long time because I was still having suicidal ideation thoughts. Eventually he set up an appointment with me but I was in a meltdown and told him I was having a nonfunctioning day. He said he didn't know what to do with that and that I should contact him when I was ready for a session. More rejection. I realized he wouldn't be able to help me and that I needed an autism therapist. Nonfunctioning days are part of autism, and not understanding that told me he wasn't right for me.

Nonfunctioning days are something I have been dealing with my entire life, I just didn't understand what they were. They definitely became more frequent after I developed CPTSD. Every few weeks I would feel like I just can't handle life today and call in sick. I felt guilty about those days because I wasn't sick, at least, not with something I could recognize and name, but I knew I needed the time off.

After a few weeks searching and not finding anyone the social worker suggested I do some therapy with her while I looked for someone else. She said she had very little experience with autism but was willing to listen and learn. We watched a few of the podcasts I had found, focusing on the ones that were run by professionals, and then she decided to teach me a skill. She was going to teach me how to manage my anxiety better. The first thing I needed to do was identify my emotions when I was anxious. I said I don't know, and she got upset with me. Then she wanted me to put a rubber band on my wrist and snap it whenever I got anxious. I told her that wasn't going to happen, I didn't need that kind of pain. She said I was being resistant, and I got angry. I tried to tell her I had trouble knowing what my feelings were, but she wasn't listening to me. Then I found out that she wasn't accepting my autism diagnosis and I told her to never contact me again.

"You are not on my side," I said.

While I was looking for another therapist I told some of them about that last session and they were horrified, but, no one had room for me, and each rejection led to a really bad meltdown. My autistic burnout was getting worse and worse. I was desperately trying to find another therapist because the lawyer the social worker had found to help me with my federal disability said I had to have a therapist. A few days later when I hadn't found one he dropped me. More meltdowns.

As I learned more and more about autism on my own, I also learned about the struggles of the autistic community, especially the high masking community that were being referred to as high functioning. The community did not like the terms high and low functioning. They feel it did a disservice to both ends of the spectrum because it minimized the struggles of high maskers, while ostracizing the low maskers. What struck me the most were suicide rates in the autistic community that were much, much, much higher than any other community, and the average life span of autistics is 54 for high masking autistics, and 39 for low maskers. These numbers are largely driven by suicide, and I understand why. Another thing that struck me was how hard it was to get diagnosed as an adult, and the lack of services for adults on the spectrum. There was agency after agency for children, and families of autistic children, but nothing for autistic adults. It is as if we cease to exist when we reached adulthood.

When I got an email saying a representative from my senator's office would be in my town I decided this would be an opportunity to advocate for the autistic community. The representative heard me out then said, "Alright, but what can I do for you? How can I help you personally? Do you need help with any federal agencies like SSDI?"

Yes I did. I had sent them paperwork twice but was not hearing back. I filled out the paperwork to get the senators staff to help me and went home with mixed feelings. Hopeful about getting my SSDI approved, and upset that I had not been able to help the community.

I was already on the private disability I had paid into through the university, it had taken several months multiple phone calls and numerous meltdowns and shut downs, but I eventually got approved. They said I needed to get approved for federal disability or they would reduce my payments. No one would help me without a therapist and primary care physician and I had neither. Eventually I spoke with an attorney from another state who told me that if SSDI didn't have enough medical evidence they would set up an interview with me before making a decision and that I didn't need to get an attorney until they had rejected me the first time.

With the help of an organization called AANE I found a therapist who specialized in both autism and C/PTSD. During our first session I knew I had struck gold. She was saying many things I had concluded, and even had answers for me about things my previous therapists were unable to tackle. My first therapist had said I would probably never be able to know when it was the CPTSD and when it was the autism that were driving my reactions when I asked him about it. This therapist knew how to differentiate between the two, and when I was being affected by one, or the other, or both. SSDI finally contacted me, I sent in the second set of paperwork they had asked for and they wanted to know if I would do an interview if needed. I said yes, and gave them my current therapists information. They never asked for an interview. Within a few days of receiving my second questionnaire, and my current therapist's assessment I was approved.

My autistic burnout was so bad that I was having trouble with basic self-care like showering, and I was often going for a week without showering. My skin was breaking out, and I looked every bit as bad as I felt. Since developing CPTSD I have been dealing with insomnia and it was now almost as bad as it was during those few months with D when I couldn't sleep. Additionally, even though I had been cooking since I was six years old, my nutrition was bad because I had such severe executive function loss that I couldn't cook. I was living off of ready to eat, and junk food. These are things I would eat when I was going through a bad emotional period for a few months, then come out of it and start eating healthy again. While I was in residential care I came to the realization that my bad eating habits when I am in an emotional low are a form of self-harm like cutting. As soon as I start to feel better junk food tastes bad to me. I realize now that during those times I also go through a mild autistic burnout and lose some of my executive function. My situation was so bad now that I was craving bad food like I never had before. I even had thoughts of eating myself to death, and I gained more weight than I ever had. Every time I started to heal something new would send me spiraling downwards. I had no capacity for dealing with the world.

One of the issues I was dealing with, that was sending me into constant overwhelm meltdown and shutdown, was my EEOC complaint. I was working with my second therapist when they contacted me about mediation with the university. My initial response was yes, because I was still hoping to find a way to go back. I loved the work. The agent advised me not to try and go back, just ask for some monetary compensation. Dr. R had warned me not to work under C again, but she hadn't told me to not go back to my job at all. I realize now that my desire to go back was also a symptom of my difficulty handling change. After a few weeks I rescinded my decision to mediate because the mediator was so demanding that I couldn't handle the pressure he was putting on me to make decisions quickly. He told me that if I sent the complaint to investigation it could take years and possibly nothing would come out of it. I told him I needed years to heal and be able to deal with it all so I was fine with that.

Two months later the EEOC contacted me for a rebuttal to my employer's response. It took three weeks for me to recover enough from the request to be able to take action. I had to go to the library because it wasn't something I could do on my phone. I bought a tablet to write this book. The library was noisy, and I had to go a few times, but got it done the last day it was due. Two weeks later the EEOC contacted me to say they were dismissing my case because my employer had offered me an accommodation, and I had a meltdown. I contacted them to try and plead my case but it didn't matter that the accommodation wasn't what I needed. As long as they offered me one they couldn't do anything. I understood at that moment why they had made the offer, it was to cover themselves. The EEOC hadn't even read the seven page response I had worked so hard to craft, all they saw was a confirmation that at some point my employer had offered an accommodation. When I got the right to sue letter in the mail I went into a horrific meltdown and subsequent shutdown that lasted the entire 30 days I had to sue. What had happened to the EEOC taking years to investigate? I was left without any recourse, I had failed again.

Chapter 23
Finding Purpose

Writing all of this has been difficult. On the days I am able to write, it is for no more than an hour, often less. There have been many days, even weeks, when I couldn't write at all. Having to relive some of those experiences has pushed me into multiple meltdowns and shutdowns. Without the support of my therapist, I would have never gotten through it. However, it has given me much insight into what has happened to me over the years, and most importantly, it has given me a sense of purpose. I never envisioned being on disability for an extended period of time, and it bothers me. Being a contributing member of society is important to me and I am struggling to envision a life without that. It took me months to realize that I would never be able to work a regular job again. The risk of another major autistic burnout is too great, and I know that I will not survive another major autistic burnout. After my attempted suicide in 2006 I was sure I would never become suicidal again. Now I know that I am more likely to become suicidal in the future if I am not very careful. I fought as hard as I could for as long as I could, and have no resilience left. I feel like I have been smashed into a million pieces. Every so often I am able to glue a few pieces back together, but no matter how many pieces I glue together I will never be as resilient as I was before.

As we age the cumulative effects of our negative experiences, the struggle to live in a world that does not operate on our terms, the world's increasing unwillingness to give us the space to operate on our terms, and the need to mask in order to succeed in life start to take their toll, and autistics become more prone to autistic burnout. Without the ability to fully heal the risk becomes incalculable.

Some days I feel like I am recovering only to crash the next day. Sometimes I feel good enough to start planning tasks to do that day but by the time I finish the first I am worn out and can't function the rest of the day. From time to time, I try and push past what my body and brain are telling me with the hopes that I can just push through this, and the results are disastrous.

Will I ever recover from this autistic burnout? I used to think I never would. Now I am starting to see some hope, but I have no idea how much longer it will take. Every time I think I have turned a corner something happens that sends me spiraling down in ways I never envisioned. I think I can recover, at least enough to manage my self-care, and a few hours of something meaningful per week, I just don't know how long it will take. One key will be finding purpose, even on a volunteer basis, so I can operate on my own terms, and not risk getting pushed off a cliff again.

Stories should end on a positive note, but for a very long time I couldn't come up with a positive ending. It was hard to completely let go of my feelings of utter failure, the suicidal thoughts, and the peace ending my life could bring. Eighteen months after returning home I was listening to a podcast. Two therapists were interviewing a transgender woman who had realized after 15 years, multiple surgeries and procedures, that she would never be able to achieve her goal of becoming a real woman, that at best she would be able to pass as a woman but she would always be a man. There was no way for her to de-transition after so many surgeries, and she was stuck with the body she had worked so hard to create but no longer gave her any relief. But she was still able to be positive about her life, and did not see herself as a failure. Listening to her made me realize maybe I'm not a failure either, maybe there is still hope. Maybe I don't need to climb another mountain to succeed. Maybe I just need to pull myself out of this ditch and keep walking, steering clear of mountains and cliffs. I put my last suicidal thoughts behind me. There's a reason I'm still alive, I just have to figure out where to go next.

PART III
A Community in Crisis

Chapter 24

When I went to speak with a representative of my state senator's office I wanted to help the autistic community because I realized that we are a community in crisis. This section is my thoughts on what needs to change to make high masking autistic lives better. While I have interacted with many other autistics and heard their thoughts on many of these issues, I am not qualified to speak for the community. These are my thoughts, and this should be seen as no more than a discussion opener, to find ways to create understanding between the autistic and allistic communities, and bring about autism acceptance. Not just for high masking autistics, but all autistics. We are after all, all human beings.

The Double Empathy Problem

Being autistic is not the problem, the problem is the double empathy problem I discussed in Part I. Because our brains are wired to operate in different ways allistics and autistics do not understand each other. This leads to misunderstandings on both sides. Because autistics are such a small minority the brunt of these misunderstandings falls on autistics. By nature of our small numbers, we interact much more with allistics and therefore end up having significantly more negative experiences. The situation is more difficult for undiagnosed autistics who have no comprehension of the source of these misunderstandings.

The Medical Community Message

Exacerbating the double empathy problem is the fact that the medical community only focuses on our deficits. In the last version of the DSM when the Spectrum was created, highly intelligent autistics went from having a syndrome to having a disorder. Next the medical community decided to include "All other learning disabilities not otherwise specified." The message given by this addition is that autism is a learning disability, rather than a neurodivergence that requires some different methods of interaction, and has different strengths. Because the medical community sees us in such a negative light, most allistic literature about autistics is negative, which leads to the general public seeing us as deficient. No one ever talks about our strengths, or our contributions to society over the millennia. High Functioning autism is described as an autistic person who is capable of living on their own without assistance. We are capable of so much more than that. Autism is not something new, but the term autism is relatively new. For tens of thousands of years autistics have lived as valuable contributing members of society. As more and more high masking autistics are getting diagnosed we are being found in all walks of life. Autism is not a mental health disorder, it is a neurodivergence. Our brains are wired differently and there are no drugs or procedures that can change that, nor should there be. Society needs us.

Autism Through the Ages

In ancient times our sensory sensitivities were an advantage. Being able to see, hear, and smell things others can't means that we were able to perceive danger before any allistics could. If a predator was creeping up, or a forest fire was burning in the distance we would be able to sense it much sooner, and would give everyone around us an advantage in escaping the fire or warding off the predator. Sensory overload would be very rare because our heightened senses are adapted to nature. What we are not adapted to is modern machines and gadgets that send us into sensory overload. Ironically we were highly instrumental in the development of these machines and gadgets.

Over time our enhanced pattern recognition, and systematic approach to analyzing things led to innovation and discovery. Many of the most renowned scientists are either confirmed, or believed to have been autistic. You may have heard of Galileo, Sir Isaac Newton, Charles Darwin, Thomas Edison, and Albert Einstein to name a few.

In 2006 Michael Fitzgerald (Ireland), claimed in an interview that "All human innovation was driven by slightly autistic people, Aspergers, and autistic people. The human race would still be sitting around in caves chattering to each other if it weren't for them." While I see the truth in that statement, where would autistic people be without allistics? We would be coming up with innovative ways of doing things but our ideas would never spread because no one would be chatting or exploring and that's how ideas spread. The human race succeeded because of the collaboration between autistics and allistics, each of us doing what we do best. We need each other to succeed.

Reality Check

Autistics are not all geniuses, or savants. Autism can be found at every IQ level, race, and skin color. For millennia, many of us have lived long productive lives. Many of our problems stem from comorbidities such as C/PTSD, OCD, and ADHD, as well as society perceptions. It is true that many autistics are more heavily impaired, but some allistics are also heavily impaired. Imagine being judged by the fact that some allistic children are born with down syndrome, and being placed in that same category. There is nothing wrong with having down syndrome, it's not something anyone should be condemned for, but would you like to be perceived and judged as being the same as a person with down syndrome when you're not? Even worse is that some more heavily impaired autistics are actually highly intelligent. Consider that they might have a lot to offer the world. New technology is allowing some nonverbal autistics to interact with the world and we are finding out many of them have a lot to offer. In 2018 Philip Reyes wrote a post about his struggles being a nonverbal autistic. In his post, he describes hating himself because of the things people would constantly say to his face, believing that because he was nonverbal, he couldn't understand them. This type of abuse is common for all autistics to a degree, but it's much worse for nonverbal autistics who are often assumed to be non-comprehending. This type of verbal abuse towards autistics is a symptom of the double empathy problem I talked about in Part I.

A Matter of Perception

Heavily impaired autistics were recognized first. It wasn't until the 1990's that the medical community started to recognize less impaired forms of autism. At the time it was called Aspergers Syndrome, and I believe we have just scratched the surface at recognizing autism in all its iterations. All autistics share a certain number of the traits and sensitivities found within The Spectrum. This is what led to the creation of The Spectrum. But we should not all be put in the same category as far as our abilities to contribute to society are concerned. By creating the spectrum in 2013 the medical community lumped us all into one category making it harder for society to recognize how diverse the autistic community is. Some of us are highly intelligent, and innovative. The world needs our intelligence and innovation. The world needs our ability to think outside the box and come up with solutions an allistic mind could not conceive. Where would electric vehicle technology, or our space program be without Elon Musk? Please see us as unique individuals, not a subpar group that needs to be relegated to the sidelines. We are not defective, we are different. We are not a tragedy; we are a much needed thread that runs through the tapestry of humanity.

The Good, the Bad, and the Ugly

One of the traits society deems as most problematic is our difficulties understanding social situations. But that inability is often replaced with enhanced pattern recognition, and increased memory. These traits have benefited humanity over the millennia, so why are we in deficit? Why not see us as other-abled rather than just impaired? If the world would stop judging us by the label autistic, and start seeing us as individuals, each with our own unique talents, abilities, and struggles, maybe we wouldn't have to hide behind a mask all the time, and suicide rates in the autistic community would come down. Suicide rates in the adult autistic community are ten times higher than in the allistic community, and are even higher in autistic children. But, how many suicides that are considered allistic, are actually high masking undiagnosed autistics? We are masters of disguise. Not because we want to deceive anyone, but because it's the only way we can currently survive in this world, but masking is sending us to an early grave. The average lifespan of a high masking autistic is 54. For low masking autistics the average lifespan is 39. This has to be resolved. We evolved together for a reason, the world needs us.

Ignored

Despite the unprecedented suicide rate in the autistic community, the extremely high rate of unemployment, and high rates of homelessness, no one is talking about these issues in main stream media. Why aren't autistic rights human rights? Why don't autistic lives matter? Why is ABA (Applied Behavior Analysis) therapy still allowed, when conversion therapy was abolished? We don't want to be living on government handouts, we want to be contributing members of society. Where is our activism? Is it possible they are sending information to main stream media but main stream media is choosing to ignore it? Or is our activism falling short? The Interagency Autism Coordinating Committee, IACC, hosts an annual conference on the welfare of autistic individuals in the United States. In 2023 the IACC focused on adults, including some of the challenges high masking autistics face. Listening to that conference, I felt seen, and heard. I saw myself in every high masking autistic adult that spoke. But there was no mainstream media coverage. How do we fix this problem? The only way we can ever fix the double empathy problem is by creating awareness in the general public. But all the discussion about autistic needs and struggles never gets to the general public. There are hundreds of podcasts about autism throughout various social media platforms. But, unless you are specifically searching for autism related content, it will never pop up on your feed.

Clashing Cultures

What we are dealing with is a clash of cultures. Understanding another person's culture can be difficult. One of my previous landlords was Korean, and his father was a handyman. Whenever something needed to be fixed his father would do the repairs. The problem was that his repairs were at best ineffective, and at worst, worse than the original problem. Whenever I would express frustration over the repairs my landlord would always respond with, "My father in his wisdom chose to do it that way."

That response would anger me because I thought he was dismissing the problem. Eventually I came to realize that because of his culture he couldn't out right say anything negative about his father, and that when he said, "My father in his wisdom chose to do it that way," he was actually agreeing with me. So, I stopped getting angry whenever he said that.

In Part I, I mentioned the difference in our communication styles. Autistics are very blunt and direct, while allistics use a more nuanced communication style. These differences lead to a lot of the misunderstandings between autistics and allistics because we are each trying to interpret what the other is saying with our own communication style. Some autistics are aware and capable of trying to understand allistic speech, others are not. Even when we try, we often fail. Since my diagnosis I have been wishing for an allistic to autistic dictionary to help me figure it all out. These differences in communication are the reason my words often come back to me as something completely different from what I said. Allistics look for nuance where there isn't any and interpret what I am saying through their own lens coming up with an interpretation that isn't there. Autistics have a similar but opposite process of taking nuanced speech and interpreting it as direct communication and misunderstanding the intent. While I was living in Israel I visited a fairly prestigious stable. They had a foreign employee who spoke English so I spent some time talking to him curious to find out what it was like to live in Israel with the status of a non-citizen, and not being Jewish. Not long after we ended our conversation the stable manager came to me and demanded that I leave because I had threatened to have their foreign worker deported. I was told to leave and never come back or I would be arrested for trespassing. No matter how much I protested and denied saying those things the manager refused to listen to me. Needless to say, I was upset, confused, and angry. Now that I understand the allistic autistic dichotomy, I finally understand how that misunderstanding happened. But after a lifetime of interactions like that I am wary of interacting with the world.

If we could all take a step back whenever we think someone has said something we perceive as rude, hurtful, threatening, or inappropriate, and just give that person the benefit of the doubt that they are a good person with good intentions the world would be much easier for everyone to navigate. Why not say to the person "This is what I heard, is that what you meant?" So many misunderstandings could be avoided if we did that. Can we just accept that some people think and express themselves differently? The vast majority of our misunderstandings come from differences in cultural backgrounds, and neurodivergence, not malice.

People get angry with me when I give them facts that contradict their feelings about something, and I get very frustrated when my facts are dismissed with "Well that's not how I feel about it." My master's degree is incomplete. Even though I was on the hydrology tract for the Master of Water Resources Program I still had to take two classes from the management list of approved courses. The first class I took was a political science class and it was an easy A because it was fact based and easy to learn. But the other options were humanities based, and I knew that many humanities classes didn't work that way. Eventually I settled on Environmental Justice. I was working as the Environment Department Incident Response Coordinator, and I thought this would help me deal with some of the citizen complaints. During the course, whenever I had to express an opinion I would back it up with facts and science because it was the only approach I was familiar with. Halfway through the course the professor told me I had to stop using science because no one understood what I was saying, and I was upsetting the other students. But I couldn't stop because it was the only way I knew to operate. Eventually I was removed from the class and ended up with a C despite finishing every homework assignment and handing in a final paper backing up all my statements with facts, and citations. I appealed, and the university sided with the professor. What I think I didn't understand at the time was that I was supposed to use my emotions to make my points. But even if I had known that I wouldn't have been able to do it. My way of understanding the world is through facts. When I hear a story I am collecting facts and analyzing them, not feeling the story. Any emotions I have from the story come from analyzing the facts. I may be wrong but I don't think that's how allistics operate. My grade upset me, but being told I wasn't allowed to use science to prove my points completely derailed me. The thought of getting a degree from a higher education institution that didn't allow the use of science made it impossible for me to continue. In fact, I think I went into an autistic burnout after those events. Knowing what I know now, I am willing to accept that feelings are more important to allistic people than facts. Can allistic people accept that facts are more important to me than feelings? Can we call a truce on this culture war, and resolve the double empathy problem?

Unemployment

Because we are perceived as less than, and judged more by our social inabilities than our other abilities 85% of autistics with college degrees are either unemployed or under employed. We struggle to do well in interviews, and interviewers tend to not like us. If we land a job we are often judged on things like how coworkers feel about us rather than how well we perform the actual job. If we disclose our autism in order to get a much needed accommodation they find a way to deny us, or get rid of us. Some industries are more autistic friendly because they recognize our superior abilities for the specific tasks they need done. Most of the fully employed autistics are in those professions do very well. The rest of the fully employed autistics are soldiering on, ignoring their needs, and heading for severe autistic burnout.

Most places of employment judge us by allistic standards of sociability. It was Einstein who allegedly said that if you judge a fish by its ability to climb trees it will always see itself as incompetent. Please stop judging us by what we can't do, and start recognizing what we **can** do. We have varying interests, so please stop pigeon holing us into certain career paths. A determined high masking autistic can learn to do any job they have a real interest in. Would you have thought that an autistic could successfully run a complaints hotline like I did for six years?

Our interests vary greatly. Spinning things and trains have never interested me, nor am I compelled to line things up all the time. But I am very interested in how the natural world works, the health effects of various chemicals on our bodies, and helping people solve their problems. Some autistics love pro sports, some love marketing, some love playing instruments, all things I have no interest in. Every sector of society would benefit from having a few autistic minds in it. After all, we successfully evolved by working together. If we can resolve the double empathy problem the sociability aspect should become less relevant.

Homelessness

Because of the low employment rate, many autistics are homeless. Autistics with mental health comorbidities are more likely to find themselves on the streets, and comorbidities are higher in the autistic community than the allistic community. Navigating disability services is very difficult and overwhelming. I had multiple meltdowns while trying to get on federal disability. Why isn't anyone helping the homeless autistics get on disability? Homelessness adds to the low life span of autistics.

Workplace Accommodations

Because we are differently abled we do need workplace accommodations. We also need better protections that would allow us to actually get the accommodations. Too often I hear people dismiss the needs of people with invisible disability. The world needs to understand that our needs are just as valid as those with visible disabilities. Denying the needs of those with invisible disabilities the accommodations they need is no different than denying someone in a wheelchair the right to a ramp. These needs will vary from autistic to autistic. This could lead to confusion and perhaps the sense that some are taking advantage of the system. The best way to address this would be to have impartial state appointed negotiators who are well versed in the issues of the disabled community who could make sure our needs are being met while ensuring employers are not being taken advantage of. Currently these things are handled internally by someone who is paid for by the employer. When the employer is paying their salary, they will side with the employer rather than the disabled employee, thereby creating a situation where the employee cannot get the accommodations they need. Employers know how to get around the current set of federal regulations. We need better regulations to protect the needs of the disabled community.

A Changing World

As the world becomes noisier, and brighter it becomes harder for us to find a space within society to exist peacefully. Every time I walk into a store, or down a crowded street, there is a strange discomfort accompanied by a buzz and fogginess in my head. It wasn't until I got diagnosed that I realized it was sensory overload.

We have been doing our best to mask and live in the allistic world. But it's getting harder and harder with ever changing social norms. Too much change is our Kryptonite. How much is too much will vary from autistic to autistic. But we all need a certain amount of consistency to thrive. One of the hardest things to deal with is the effects of social media on society that leads to constantly changing societal demands. Imagine if that eye blinking sequence I talked about in part II kept changing, how would that affect your ability to get it right? People's lives get destroyed for saying the wrong thing on social media. We can avoid social media but we can't avoid the spill over into real life. One thing I can guarantee is that as an autistic I will say something someone will find offensive every time I open my mouth. The thought that some people will find something in my book offensive and try to cancel it terrifies me, but it's too important, so I will put it out there and do my best to deal with any fallout. Not because I think I am saying anything offensive, but because all too often things I say gets twisted into something completely different than what I said. Do I need to keep hiding away, afraid to talk to anyone just to survive? Can everyone stop being so hyperbolic and judgmental all the time? True autism acceptance will be achieved when we can live as our authentic selves and be accepted in all walks of life. Right now, we are either masking all the time, or in hiding. It's the only two options we have besides suicide, and it's killing us no matter what approach we take. We need some stability of expectations, acceptance and understanding.

Change is happening at an ever increasing rate as if we are trying to keep our global rate of change in sync with the expansion of the universe. One hundred years ago companies advertised by saying things like, "Established in 1XXX," promoting how long they had been around to show how reliable they were. Today it's all about "new and improved." New gadgets, new apps, new social media platforms, new movies, new flavors, new options, new everything. It's exhausting! The world won't change how it does business because of us. But can the world try and understand the toll it's putting on us, be a little more understanding, and realize that it is getting harder, and harder, to cope with all the change? Please stop judging us so harshly when we struggle to handle change. All this change is making it harder to adjust when we really need to. I heard one autistic describe the meltdown she will go into if she is going out to dinner with friends and they decide to change the venue at the last minute. This has never happened to me though I will sometimes go into overwhelm when a change of venues occurs, depending on other factors. We are not being difficult when we object to change, we are expressing our needs. One time when I organized a hike a few people decided in the middle of the hike that they wanted to take a different route because they didn't like the route I had chosen. They got angry with me and left the hike when I refused to change the route. I didn't understand why they joined the hike if they didn't like the route I had chosen, and I ended up being ostracized by a lot of people over that incident.

Sensory Seeking Autism

There are some autistics who are sensory seeking. They are on the hypo end of the spectrum. They have their own set of issues and needs that I cannot address because I have no experience with that end of the spectrum, but their needs should be included in any solutions society comes up with.

Autistic Socializing

Contrary to myth many autistics enjoy socializing, just in smaller groups, one on one, or through an activity. Not being able to socialize because we make mistakes and are shunned is very painful for most autistics. Not everyone does this, and I am very grateful to the ballroom dancing community for their acceptance. But this should be the majority, not the exception.

The Need for Adult Diagnosis

There are still many undiagnosed autistic adults, mostly those who, like me, were born at a time when it was impossible for a high masking autistic to get diagnosed as child. Some have self-diagnosed and are seeking diagnosis but can't get access to diagnosis, others don't know they are autistic. It's very difficult to find someone who is qualified to do the diagnosis who will evaluate an adult. This leaves self-diagnosed adults in limbo, unable to know if they really are autistic or not.

There seems to be an attitude of 'you made it this far so you should be fine'. I hope my story debunks that attitude. Autistics are often on the precipice of a cliff their entire adult lives, and being undiagnosed makes the situation more precarious. For women this can be even more problematic as we enter menopause. I wonder if part of the reason my last autistic burnout was so bad is related to menopause.

We need more opportunities for adults to get evaluated, and it should be covered by our health insurance. The cost of diagnosis is another reason many are left in limbo because they can't afford to pay for the evaluation. We also need better criteria for autistic women who often present differently than autistic men. Then there are the ones who haven't realized they are autistic. We need to find ways to diagnose them before they are in crisis, or worse. Perhaps a questionnaire aimed at figuring out who might be autistic and need evaluation in doctors' offices, when people sign up for unemployment, and other social services. Many undiagnosed autistics avoid doctors because we feel dismissed whenever we go see one.

Autism and Therapy

There needs to be better oversight over who can work with autistic individuals within the mental health profession. Autism is extremely complex, and many autistics have comorbidities that add to the complexity. Too many of us end up trying to get help from therapists who lack the qualifications to help us. Bad therapy can be worse than no therapy because it can be very damaging to have a therapist say things like "you want to be depressed" or "you are being resistant" when being asked to do something you simply cannot do. We don't have dermatologists doing heart surgeries. Our mental health, everyone's mental health, should be protected from therapists who are unqualified to treat our conditions. In order to work with a certain condition a therapist should have a minimal amount of specific education pertaining to that condition. The way things work now it's all on the client to figure it out, and most mental health clients lack the understanding of how therapy works to know what to look for until we have been seriously traumatized. I have heard from many autistics who have been so badly abused in therapy that they refuse to ever see another therapist.

We need better standardization of mental health diagnosis. The fact that autistic women regularly get misdiagnosed with borderline personality disorder, or bipolar disorder shows how ineffective the current system is. If a medical doctor misdiagnoses a patient they run the risk of losing their license and/or get a malpractice suit. But mental health care providers misdiagnose and/or under-diagnose clients regularly with no repercussions.

This book is about adults, but, there is one issue pertaining to autistic children that I cannot keep quiet about. Many autistic children are subject to ABA therapy from a young age to "correct" their "bad" behavior. ABA therapy was created in part by Dr. Ivar Lovaas who also had a hand in creating gay conversion therapy, and they use the same principles. While electric shocks have been discontinued in recent years, ABA remains abusive and disempowering. ABA is obedience training and autistic children are taught to behave the way you would train a circus animal to do tricks. These children have no understanding of why they are required to do these things because the explanations they are given often don't make sense to them. Some ABA therapists believe they are helping these children, but the fact is that they are doing damage. These children are asked to do things they find extremely painful to do, and denied things they need to do in order to self-regulate such as stimming during these sessions. The result is autistics who have no ability to think for themselves, they are people pleasing automatons who have been trained to ignore their own needs and need to create scripts in their head to navigate the labyrinth of behaviors they were taught because they have no understanding of what they are actually doing. All they know is that if they get it wrong they will be punished. ABA needs to be abolished. There are multiple other modalities that can help autistics without taking away their sense of self, individual needs, and ability to think independently. Yes, there are behaviors that need to be stopped. But why is the child self-injuring? Why is the child suddenly hitting everyone around them? Instead of punishing them to the point of them being afraid to do it, why not figure out if there's a sensory issue that's causing the problem and rectify it? Or teach them a less injurious way to stim? Gay conversion therapy was never about helping gay people, it was about changing them to make heteronormative people more comfortable around them. ABA therapy is not about helping autistic children, it's about changing them into something allistics are more comfortable with. It's time to end the sanctioned abuse of autistic children.

Adult Autistic Services

When I got diagnosed Dr. R told me that now I would be able to get the help I needed. But there is no help available. We need services for autistic adults in crisis. It took me two years to be able to clean my kitchen floor as I was going through this last autistic burnout. I will spare the rest of the horrors of my abysmal housekeeping abilities during that period. I know how to clean, finding the energy to clean was, and still is, the problem. How my house looks absolutely disgusts me, but I am so limited with what I can do in one day. It would have been helpful to have someone come in once a month, even once every other month and do some cleaning. There are so many agencies for autistic children and their families, but autistic adults don't seem to exist when it comes to services. Just because we are considered high functioning doesn't mean we don't need help through the more difficult periods of our lives. Hopefully, when society starts to change, we won't end up in such severe crisis as often. But there will always be a need for help through the harder times.

Acceptance

Most importantly we need society to accept us for who we are and meet us half way. Constantly masking takes a toll, and we need to be able to drop the mask without suffering dire consequences. The only way to achieve that is through acceptance, and the only way to have acceptance is through awareness. The only way to create awareness is for our voices to be heard.

Summary of Needs

- Acceptance for who we are so we don't need to mask, or hide all the time.
- Recognition of our strengths.
- Public awareness of our struggles and needs.
- Appropriate workplace accommodations, and more stringent regulations surrounding workplace accommodations.
- More access to diagnosis opportunities for adults.
- Adult autism diagnosis covered by health insurance.
- Assistance with federal disability applications to reduce homelessness.
- Services for adults in crisis.
- Regulated therapy services.
- Opportunities to socialize through activities.

R. Horowitz

Ruth currently resides in the United States.

Milton Keynes UK
Ingram Content Group UK Ltd.
UKHW041307151124
2882UKWH00046B/217